PASTORAL COUNSELING IN WORK CRISES

Henry Haskell Rightor

An Introduction for Both Lay and Ordained Ministers

Judson Press ® Valley Forge

PASTORAL COUNSELING IN WORK CRISES

Unless otherwise indicated, Bible quotations in this volume are in accordance with the Revised Standard Version of the Bible, copyrighted 1946, 1952, 1971, 1973 © by the Division of Christian Education of the National Council of the Churches of Christ in the United States of America, and are used by permission.

Other versions of the Bible quoted in this book are:

The Holy Bible, King James Version.

The New English Bible, Copyright © The Delegates of the Oxford University Press and the Syndics of the Cambridge University Press, 1961, 1970.

Library of Congress Cataloging in Publication Data

Rightor, Henry Haskell.
    Pastoral counseling in work crises.

    Bibliography: pp. 75-78.
    Includes index.
    1. Pastoral counseling.   2. Vocational guidance.   I. Title.
BV4012.2.R53   253.5   78-22007
ISBN 0-8170-0814-4

The name JUDSON PRESS is registered as a trademark in the U.S. Patent Office.
Printed in the U.S.A. ⊕

Dedicated
to the memory of
Theodore Otto Wedel
1892–1970
Friend, Pastor, Mentor,
Teacher, Theologian

Acknowledgments

There are many individuals whose counsel and whose writings have been indispensable to me in the preparation of this book. Natalie Harris Cabot Neagle, together with her late husband, Hugh Cabot, first introduced me to the problems and opportunities of "the healthy aging" when they were directing the New England Center for the Aging. That was in 1965 when I was a Merrill Fellow at the Harvard Divinity School, and she had already published *You Can't Count on Dying* (Boston: Houghton Mifflin Company, 1961). A few years later Bernard Haldane, now of Seattle, Washington, but then with Bernard Haldane Associates of Washington, D.C., showed me the scope of work crises in our society. Barton M. Lloyd, former director of the Mid-Atlantic Career Center in Washington, D.C., and now with the New England Career Development Center in Wellesley Hills, Massachusetts, afforded me some practical experience serving on the staff of several career guidance workshops he was leading. Richard N. Bolles has been unusually helpful both as an author and personally as director of an extended Life/Work Shop, sponsored by the National Career Development Project of United Ministries in Higher Education, which I attended in the summer of 1976.

There are other individuals to whom I am more than grateful.

One of them is John C. Crystal of McLean, Virginia, co-author with Bolles of the manual *Where Do I Go from Here with My Life?* (New York: The Seabury Press, Inc., 1974). The writings which I have mentioned here in addition to those cited in the body of this book should constitute an ample beginning bibliography for anyone interested in investigating the field of counseling in work crises. For those who may wish to go further, there is an extraordinarily full bibliography and a listing of sources for professional help in the appendices of Bolles's *What Color Is Your Parachute? A Practical Manual for Job-Hunters and Career Changers* (Berkeley: Ten Speed Press, 1977), hereafter referred to simply as *What Color Is Your Parachute?* from which I have quoted extensively in the pages that follow.

Among the institutions to which I am indebted is, first of all, the Virginia Theological Seminary, which gave me the sabbatical leave during which I did much of the study that lies behind this work. I appreciate, too, the assistance I have received from the staffs of the American Association of Retired Persons and the Ethel Percy Andrus Gerontology Center, University of Southern California, Los Angeles.

Henry Haskell Rightor

Virginia Theological Seminary
Alexandria, Virginia

Contents

1

An Introduction to Pastoral Counseling in Work Crises

A PARABLE—WITH LIMITATIONS

Once there was an island people who depended for their existence on their ability to navigate the sea about them. They were a proud people, however, and their pride led them to pretend that the many shoals and reefs surrounding their island did not exist. Even when their boats actually ran aground on the submerged shoals and reefs, they would not ask for help. Instead, they pretended that they had anchored there to fish. This attitude made their lives very hazardous.

One day, one of their leaders narrowly escaped drowning when his boat struck a reef. When he finally made shore, he called a meeting of the island people and proclaimed that he had had enough of this pretense. He said that they all knew that the island waters abounded in shoals and reefs that were a source of great harm to them all. He went on to say that navigational charts and maps were available to help them avoid these dangers. Moreover, he said, he was going to begin organizing groups to help the people use these charts and maps and to rescue others who would continue to run aground in heavy seas in spite of the help available to them.

The parable is intended to illustrate the hazards of unacknowledged work crises. All parables have limitations—they have been compared to a dog walking on three legs[1]—and this one is no exception. For instance, the work crisis which often accompanies retirement can be one of the most common and destructive types. Yet there are some healthy individuals and couples who do intentionally drop anchor and fish after retirement—and enjoy it! Their number is relatively small, however, in comparison to those who pretend that this and other work crises do not exist in spite of the problems those crises cause. The fact remains that a severe strain is sometimes put on the marital bond when a healthy husband, who has worked all his married life, is suddenly retired. There must be *some* truth in the old jest in which a wife protests: "I married you for better or worse, but not for lunch!"

THE SCOPE OF WORK CRISES TO BE CONSIDERED

The inquiry that lies behind this book was originally limited to pastoral counseling in the work crises brought on by the retirement, or approaching retirement, of the healthy aging. "Healthy aging" is a shorthand description of persons past middle age who are able to work part-time if not full-time, within if not without their homes, on a pay or volunteer basis, as a disciplined expression of their creative energies.

The scope of the study was broadened when it soon became apparent that the work crisis of the healthy aging facing retirement does not differ *in theory* from the work crisis of younger people; and that an investigation of pastoral counseling in any work crisis would suffer if it were limited to healthy persons in a single age category.[2] As a result, the work crises considered here will include situations as diverse as young people attempting to enter the job market for the first time, older women trying to reenter it, release from employment, job dissatisfaction, and compulsory retirement of the healthy aging.

It is safe to say that the numbers of work crises in all the

[1] Theodore O. Wedel, who enjoyed writing parables himself, wrote in *The Gospel in a Strange, New World* (Philadelphia: The Westminster Press, 1963), p. 99: "'All analogies,' so reads a Jesuit proverb, 'walk on three legs.'"

[2] This statement is not intended to deprecate the practice of career counseling and guidance limited to persons within certain age limits. An example of such limitation is the offering of seminars to persons fifty to sixty-five years of age who are still employed, by Action for Independent Maturity, an arm of the American Association of Retired Persons.

categories mentioned are rapidly increasing in our society. The increasing number of unemployed persons reflects this. Statistics alone, however, do not always reflect the increasing number of healthy aging who are reaching retirement age or the increasingly short tenure of younger people holding jobs. Nowhere is there any computation of the number who are suffering acutely because of their dissatisfaction with the jobs they are presently holding.

It would be difficult to determine the number of individuals and families in a congregation who are affected by work crises at any given time. The normal tendency of those involved, as well as those who are not immediately involved, is to pretend that the work crises do not exist. One reason for the pretense is that such a crisis is often considered a sign of defeat. Therefore, it is looked on as demeaning to the persons involved whereas, perhaps, a bereavement as a crisis is not seen that way. Another reason for this pretense may be that the congregation senses that the pastor is not aware of the extent or the significance of their work crises. This, if the congregation be correct, could mean that the pastor may not be prepared to deal with work crises in the helpful way that pastors have always dealt with other crises, such as those precipitated by a bereavement.

THE PURPOSE OF THIS BOOK

This book is not designed to make pastors experts in the field of career guidance. Such specialization would run counter to the author's conviction that an ordained pastor's unique value rests partly, at least, on the fact that the parish minister remains almost "the last of the generalists" available to a great many people. The purpose of this book is, rather, to foster a climate of opinion that will encourage ordained and lay pastors to recognize the existence of work crises throughout their congregations. Pastors are a conscientious lot; and once they recognize the need, they will equip themselves to deal with people in work crises as they deal with people in other crises:

1. by offering supportive counseling themselves;
2. by making materials for self-help available;
3. by enlisting on some occasions lay pastors who could, because of their present situations or similar experiences in the past, provide additional support and stimulation to the counselees; and

    4. by referring counselees to specialists in the field where such referral is indicated.[3]

When pastors begin to recognize the existence of work crises in their congregations and identify with these crises, it will not take long for the congregational climate of opinion to change, also. Work crises will no longer be the forbidden subject they are today, and pastoral counseling will be sought and provided.

Surely counseling in work crises comes within the purview of the mission given every Christian pastor by Him who said, "I am come that they might have life, and that they might have it more abundantly" (John 10:10*b*, KJV), or "I have come that men may have life, and may have it in all its fullness" (NEB).

[3] For more on this, see chapters 4 and 5.

Illustrations, Definition, and a Framework for Pastoral Counseling in Work Crises

2

TWO ILLUSTRATIONS OF PASTORAL COUNSELING IN WORK CRISES

My introduction to pastoral counseling in work crises came almost twenty-five years ago when I was serving as a parish minister. An adult education group in the parish had completed four months' study of the book of Ephesians, using as a guide Theodore O. Wedel's commentary on the book in *The Interpreter's Bible.* Canon Wedel, then warden of the Washington Cathedral's College of Preachers, had just finished leading a weekend conference with the group on Ephesians.

It was late Sunday afternoon in the spring, and a backyard cookout was being given for the group by one of its members. I was chatting informally with Canon Wedel and George, a member of the study group. George had been for several years district sales manager for a large corporation which manufactured a nationally known product. The following unforgettable conversation took place:

George: A few minutes ago, Canon Wedel, you seemed quite interested in my work. What I did not tell you is that it is about to do me in.

Canon Wedel: How do you mean?

George:	I mean that the company assigns me a sales quota each year. I strain everything I've got to make the quota—and the next year they raise it. I do the same thing the next year—and then they raise the quota again, and I have to meet it again. I don't know how long I can keep on doing this. It is hard on me, and it is hard on my wife who has to live with me.
Canon Wedel:	Do you see any chance of the company changing this policy?
George:	No, I don't.
Canon Wedel	*(thoughtfully):* George, what is the worst thing that could happen to you and your wife if you walked off that job? Seriously, what is the *very* worst thing that could *possibly* happen to you if you just quit?
George:	Well, I don't know. . . . I guess the very worst thing would be that we might both starve to death.
Canon Wedel:	George, how many people have you known *personally* who have starved to death?
George:	Well . . . I don't think I have known anyone personally who has starved to death.
Canon Wedel:	Have you known anyone personally, George, who has died of bleeding ulcers or heart attacks?
George:	Oh! All my friends go that way!
Canon Wedel:	George, is it possible that you are worrying about the wrong thing?
George:	*(Silence.)*

The case has a sad ending. George stayed on the job and died about two years later from a series of heart attacks.

Very recently, when I was beginning to write this book, I was privy to another case of pastoral counseling in a work crisis. Fortunately, the second case has a happy ending.

Mrs. Markham, let us call her, is the secretary of a colleague of mine at the seminary where I teach. She has an office very near mine, and she knows of my interest in work crises. When I passed her office one morning, Mrs. Markham called me in to get my reaction to a telephone conversation she had just had with her friend, Karen. Karen worked as an administrative assistant in a local company. She was separated but not divorced from her husband and had the care of their two children. Her telephone call of a few minutes earlier was still very much on Mrs. Markham's mind.

Karen:	I have just been given three weeks' notice by my boss! I don't know what the hell I'm going to do! Three weeks to find a job, and I haven't been on a job interview for fifteen years! And you know I don't have any money!
Mrs. Markham:	Karen, first of all, shut up and calm down and listen to me! You are not going to believe this now, but it is probably the best possible thing that could have happened.
Karen:	Maybe, but you don't have two kids and no job.
Mrs. Markham:	Karen, tell me how it happened and why.
Karen:	Well, the company is having a hard time financially and will be reducing its staff. I am the highest paid administrative assistant—in addition, I have been criticized for wearing slacks on the job.
Mrs. Markham:	Well, don't worry. You will have a job before you know it and be better off than before. I'll find out what employment office the seminary uses and ask some of the other secretaries which agencies they would recommend. I'll call back and fill you in just as soon as possible. Just don't worry.

I told Mrs. Markham that I thought she was right to try to calm Karen down, even if it meant being a little rough with her, and that I also thought it was a good idea to support her by putting her to work on a new job right away. As for any suggestions I might have, the local office of the Mid-Atlantic Career Center would be a good place for Karen to go for a fresh assessment of her skills and the kind of work where she might find the most satisfaction using them. I also told her that it might be a good idea to buy a copy of *What Color Is Your Parachute?*[1] at the seminary bookstore as she left the office that afternoon. If she would give the book to Karen on her way home, it could give her the confidence she needed at that point. Finally, I suggested that Karen call her lawyer for his advice if she had a formal separation agreement with her husband.

[1] Richard N. Bolles, *What Color Is Your Parachute?* (Berkeley, Calif.: Ten Speed Press, 1977).

Karen's work crisis was very brief. Mrs. Markham called her back within an hour, giving her the names of two good employment agencies and the Mid-Atlantic Career Center. (Karen rejected the idea of calling a lawyer, saying that she knew her husband would sign nothing and that he would be more likely to leave town than provide more support, especially if he knew she was in trouble.)

Before the day was over, Karen had made an appointment for a job interview the next morning through one of the employment agencies. She read most of *What Color Is Your Parachute?* that evening. The next morning she was offered a job, which she subsequently took. She had enough confidence by morning, however, to hold off accepting the offer until she could interview two other prospective employers and be very firm about her job description and salary range.

These two cases of pastoral counseling in work crises have been selected for several reasons:

1. George's case shows how a work cr. is resulting from job dissatisfaction can literally be a matter of life and death.

2. A good pastor, like Canon Wedel, takes work crises very seriously, so much so that he would risk confrontation with a counselee who knew that he was genuinely concerned.

3. George's case illustrates that a work crisis can go on for a number of years without resolution; in Karen's case, however, the crisis was resolved in a few hours.

4. Opportunities for pastoral counseling in work crises arise at unlikely times—for instance, at a backyard cookout or during a spontaneous telephone call.

5. The task of the ordained pastor is often to support a lay pastor such as Mrs. Markham who is doing the actual counseling in a work crisis.

6. There is nothing arcane about pastoral counseling in work crises; it is the kind of counseling most pastors are accustomed to giving in many other kinds of crises.

7. Negatively, it should be noted that George did not share with his regular pastor the pain associated with his work life. I had shown an interest in his Christian education, but not in the way he spent his working hours. Karen did not turn to her ordained pastor either. Instead, she turned to a Christian lay person whom she knew would understand what it is like to find yourself suddenly without regular employment.

One case of job dissatisfaction and another of sudden firing in no way cover the broad range of work crises. The crisis can be especially severe when a student, graduating from school or college, faces the job market for the first time. The same is true when a woman whose children are now in school desperately wants and needs to get back into work outside her home, or when vigorous men and women face compulsory retirement while they still have financial needs or a need to express their creative skills.

All of these situations, together with variations on them, are within the scope of work crises; pastoral counseling, by both lay and ordained pastors, could be helpful—or perhaps vital. If the behavior of people in other crises is a valid indicator, then persons would seek pastoral counseling in work crises as well if it were known that the pastor were equipped and open to offering support in that area.

A DEFINITION OF WORK CRISES

A person who is "facing a new life task" is in a "crisis," according to Erik H. Erikson. Erikson goes on to say: "A new life task presents a *crisis* whose outcome can be a successful graduation, or alternatively, an impairment of the life cycle which will aggravate future crisis." [2]

It must be quickly acknowledged that the "crises" Erikson was referring to were the eight "developmental crises" he locates in every individual's life—crises which arise from such inevitable human events as infancy or adolescence. [3] In this book I have taken the liberty of extending Erikson's definition of "developmental crises" to include "accidental crises" as well. "Accidental" crises differ from "developmental" ones in that no particular accident can be anticipated in a particular person's development; and "accidental crises" are precipitated by such unexpected or arbitrary events as the loss of a job or a personal relationship that satisfied what one considered a basic need. [4]

[2] Erik H. Erikson, *Young Man Luther* (New York: W. W. Norton & Co., Inc., 1962), p. 254.

[3] Erikson sets out his eight developmental crises fully in *Childhood and Society*, 2nd ed. (New York: W. W. Norton & Co., Inc., 1963), pp. 247-274.

[4] For an excellent amplification of the difference between "accidental" and "developmental" crises, see Howard J. Clinebell, Jr., *Basic Types of Pastoral Counseling* (Nashville: Abingdon Press, 1966), pp.158-160. This and all other quotations from Clinebell's book are used by permission. Clinebell also outlines here the contribution Gerald Caplan has made to the dynamics of crises in general in *Principles of Preventive Psychiatry* (New York: Basic Books, Inc., Publishers, 1964), pp. 26-55.

It is helpful to consider all work crises together, whether the crises are generated by the advent of a new "developmental" stage, such as adolescence or young adulthood, or whether they are generated by "accidental" events. Erikson's definition of a crisis fits both kinds, for in both a person is "facing a new life task."

In the first case given in this chapter, Canon Wedel confronted George with the probability that he had to face a new life task if he was going to survive. Unfortunately, George was either unable or unwilling to meet the challenge of a new task. Karen, on the other hand, heeded the advice to face the new life task and to face it promptly. The experience she had gained in a work crisis when she had interviewed for a job fifteen years earlier was transferable to this new crisis, although she was in a very different situation. Her counselor also provided her with new resources and the support that enabled her to meet the new life task with the assurance and aplomb that contributed to a happy resolution of the crisis.

A CONCEPTUAL FRAMEWORK FOR COUNSELING IN WORK CRISES

The "identity crisis" of late adolescence and early adulthood was first identified and described by Erik H. Erikson.[5] No attempt will be made here to restate Erikson's definition of the identity crisis, which is readily available in the author's own terms.[6] It is sufficient for the purpose of this book to state that Erikson often says, in his delineation of that crisis, that one aspect of a person's resolution of the identity crisis is the development of that person's ability to enter into mature work and love relationships. In one place he refers to "that particular combination of work and love which alone verifies our identity and confirms it."[7] Elsewhere he acknowledges his indebtedness to Freud for this formula:

> Freud was once asked what he thought a normal person should be able to do well. The questioner probably expected a complicated answer. But Freud, in the curt way of his old days, is reported to have said: "Lieben und arbeiten" (to love and to work). It pays to ponder on this simple formula . . . we may ponder, but we cannot improve on "the professor's" formula.[8]

[5] The fact that the phrase "identity crisis" has been popularly misused in recent years probably comes as no surprise to Professor Erikson, who himself has said that "a man who inspires new ideas has little power to restrict them to the area of his original intentions" (Erikson, *Young Man Luther*, p. 21).

[6] *Ibid.,* p. 14.

[7] *Ibid.,* p. 217.

[8] Erikson, *Childhood and Society*, pp. 264-265.

It is suggested here that Freud's formula of the ability "to love and to work," which Erikson developed as a mark of the resolution of the identity crisis, can enable a counselor to conceptualize what is happening when a healthy counselee is involved in a work crisis. An adolescent or young adult who is unable to work or to find work which is satisfying is likely to remain in a state of identity diffusion and require support by the counselor or others until the counselee is able to engage in a mature work relationship, although he or she may already have succeeded in achieving a mature love relationship.

A healthy older person who has previously achieved a mature work relationship may well *return* to a state of identity diffusion, comparable to the adolescent's, if his or her work relationship no longer exists. Examples of the dissolution of the work relationship of a healthy adult are dismissal from a job, obsolescence of a job, release because of an employer's financial difficulties, or retirement. If the person is a wife and mother whose principal work has been the maintenance of a household for her husband and children, her work relationship might no longer exist when the children are no longer dependent on her, when there is divorce, or when her husband dies. Similarly, a healthy older person would be *threatened* with the return to a state of identity diffusion by the approaching termination of a work relationship through retirement, job dissatisfaction, or other reasons.

In summary, the conceptual framework for counseling persons in work crises could be described as the recognition that one aspect of an adult's identity is attained through the achievement of mature work and love relationships; further, one must understand that the maintenance of an adult identity depends on the maintenance of *continuing* work and love relationships, although not necessarily the *same* ones. Therefore, when a healthy person is confronted or threatened by a work crisis, he is confronted or threatened with a relapse into an identity crisis comparable to that of late adolescence.[9] This suggests that the counseling task includes support from the counselor and others, similar in some respects to the support given a

[9] I am not aware that Erikson has actually said that the process by which an identity crisis is resolved can also be reversed. He implies as much, however, when he says of Martin Luther that "the suddenly changed course of his life endangers the identity which he had won as a lecturer and preacher" (Erikson, *Young Man Luther*, p. 221). Richard N. Bolles, *op. cit.,* p. 222, refers to studies of retired clergy and military personnel and mentions their "role confusion" and "temporary symptoms (typical of regression)" following retirement.

late adolescent in an identity crisis. The older counselee's pathway to a new work relationship becomes simpler and more hopeful, however, when there is the realization that he or she has, like Karen, successfully traveled that way before.

tory chapter of this book to
rises in our society among
vay to compute the number
satisfied with their jobs are
figures of all kinds are
est the magnitude of the

mate the number of healthy
substantial segment of the
and voluntary retirement of
ig more common, they are
work crises. If only a small
vork crises and needed and
be awesome. According to
over sixty-five are healthy;
ick or senile, the remaining
following report also leaves
over sixty-five and their
e rapidly increasing:

ulation has also been changing
4 percent of the nation's 76
r. Forty years later, although
l only 5.4 percent of the total
ne out of 10 Americans (9.9

es valid, the proportion of the
0 as the baby-boom cohort of
s senior citizen status. It can be
lerly of the year 2020 will be 13

n, among young people in
b market for the first time,
s beginning to be widely
ew York Times published a
Survey of Education and
that section Frank J. Prial

(Washington, D.C.: Population
7.

3

The Pastor as Counselor in Work Crises

THE PASTOR'S UNIQUE CONTRIBUTIONS: THEOLOGY AND EXPERIENCE

The parallel nature of mature love and work relationships has been referred to in the preceding chapter. It was pointed out that resolution of the young adult's identity crisis is marked by the achievement of these two types of relationships, which then run side by side throughout a healthy person's life unless the love or the work relationship, or both, break down through some accidental event. In the crisis which follows, or which threatens to follow, there is the likelihood of a return to a state of identity diffusion.

Christian theology has very often made the pastor adept at counseling individuals or couples when their love relationships have been strained or broken. The pastor knows, for instance, that all relationships fall short of the ideal again and again, and often are broken—but the pastor is also aware that they can be reborn and made bright and new, again and again. The Christian pastor also knows that a love relationship may be finally dissolved through divorce or the death of a loved one. The pastor's theology is again standing by, however, with the good news that God is loving and forgiving and offers men and women the opportunity to begin again,

21

in the hope that this beginning will be wiser than the o

It may well be that theology does not even stop there
knows that while Christian love relationships incl
relationships, they go far beyond that; they also include r
with any caring, supportive community "where two
gathered together in my name" (Matthew 18:20a, au
phrase).

There is no need to labor the applicability of the sa
to work relationships. Unsatisfactory work relationships
renewed; the worker and the job may also be reunited
neither of these eventualities is possible, a new work rela
be begun, here, too, perhaps, with more wisdom than v
previously.

The theology of work does not stop here either. I
pastor that work is not restricted to the "nine-to-
remunerative jobs ordinarily associated with "work." As
disciplined expression of a person's creative drive, w
place at a stove or at an easel, in a shop or in a garden. Ne
it can be caring for one's own or ministering to other

Finally, a pastoral counselor in the Judeo-Christ
has a distinct advantage over a counselor in other tra
pastor knows *why* people need both love and work
This pastor knows that men and women are made in
God, who first loved us and created us. Therefore, our
work are not demeaning and not to be left to people
choice but to be servants or slaves. Our loving and ou
our grateful responses to God who allows us to share i
his creation. This may *lead* us to service, but it is work "i

The pastor must allow, however, for counselees w
difficulty with a Christian theology of work than th
Christian theology of love. Their difficulty may be
pervasive misunderstanding of the biblical accoun
punishment after he disobeyed God in the garden of E
the pastor can throw the needed light on the Genesi

---

[1] I am still embarrassed over a conversation I had with a young n
where I had served for eight years, and where she had been teachi
school. She told me that she would not be able to do any church wor
she was expecting another child; and this meant that she would the
two very small children. After eight years I had failed to communic
that there is no higher expression of Christian "church work" tha
children.

THE INCREASING NEED FOR COUNS

Reference was made in the introdu
the rapidly increasing number of work
healthy persons of all ages. There is no
accurately; even those who are acutely d
still listed as employed. Statistics an
available, however, which clearly sug
problem.

It is possible, for instance, to approx
persons over sixty-five. They constitute
healthy aging; and with both compulsory
men and women over sixty-five becomi
becoming more and more susceptible to
proportion of the healthy aging were in
sought counseling, their number would
most estimates, 80 percent of all persons
only 10 percent of them are classified as
10 percent are infirm or housebound. The
no doubt that the number of people
proportion to the total population will

> The proportion of elderly in the U.S. po
> throughout the century. In 1900 abou
> million people were 65 years old or ov
> their numbers had tripled, they were st
> population. By 1970, however, about
> percent) were elderly.
>
> No matter which fertility projection pro
> aged will increase between 2010 and 20
> the late 1940's and the early 1950's reach
> reasonably expected that the 40 million e
> to 15 percent of U.S. population.[4]

At the other end of the age spectru
work crises because they are facing the j
the need for counseling and guidance
recognized. On November 16, 1976, the
special section, Section 11, entitled "Fa
Career Development." On the first page
wrote this in a lead article:

[4] "The Elderly in America" in *Population Bulleti*
Reference Bureau, Inc., 1975), vol. 30, no. 3, pp.

3

The Pastor as Counselor in Work Crises

THE PASTOR'S UNIQUE CONTRIBUTIONS: THEOLOGY AND EXPERIENCE

The parallel nature of mature love and work relationships has been referred to in the preceding chapter. It was pointed out that resolution of the young adult's identity crisis is marked by the achievement of these two types of relationships, which then run side by side throughout a healthy person's life unless the love or the work relationship, or both, break down through some accidental event. In the crisis which follows, or which threatens to follow, there is the likelihood of a return to a state of identity diffusion.

Christian theology has very often made the pastor adept at counseling individuals or couples when their love relationships have been strained or broken. The pastor knows, for instance, that all relationships fall short of the ideal again and again, and often are broken—but the pastor is also aware that they can be reborn and made bright and new, again and again. The Christian pastor also knows that a love relationship may be finally dissolved through divorce or the death of a loved one. The pastor's theology is again standing by, however, with the good news that God is loving and forgiving and offers men and women the opportunity to begin again, in the hope that this beginning will be wiser than the one before.

It may well be that theology does not even stop there. The pastor knows that while Christian love relationships include sexual relationships, they go far beyond that; they also include relationships with any caring, supportive community "where two or three are gathered together in my name" (Matthew 18:20a, author's paraphrase).

There is no need to labor the applicability of the same theology to work relationships. Unsatisfactory work relationships may also be renewed; the worker and the job may also be reunited; and where neither of these eventualities is possible, a new work relationship may be begun, here, too, perhaps, with more wisdom than was exercised previously.

The theology of work does not stop here either. It informs the pastor that work is not restricted to the "nine-to-five" or the remunerative jobs ordinarily associated with "work." As long as it is a disciplined expression of a person's creative drive, work can take place at a stove or at an easel, in a shop or in a garden. Needless to say, it can be caring for one's own or ministering to others.[1]

Finally, a pastoral counselor in the Judeo-Christian tradition has a distinct advantage over a counselor in other traditions. This pastor knows *why* people need both love and work relationships. This pastor knows that men and women are made in the image of God, who first loved us and created us. Therefore, our love and our work are not demeaning and not to be left to people who have no choice but to be servants or slaves. Our loving and our working are our grateful responses to God who allows us to share in his love and his creation. This may *lead* us to service, but it is work "in his service."

The pastor must allow, however, for counselees who have more difficulty with a Christian theology of work than they do with a Christian theology of love. Their difficulty may be the result of pervasive misunderstanding of the biblical account of Adam's punishment after he disobeyed God in the garden of Eden. However, the pastor can throw the needed light on the Genesis story, which

---

[1] I am still embarrassed over a conversation I had with a young matron in a parish where I had served for eight years, and where she had been teaching in the Sunday school. She told me that she would not be able to do any church work the next year, as she was expecting another child; and this meant that she would then have the care of two very small children. After eight years I had failed to communicate my conviction that there is no higher expression of Christian "church work" than caring for one's children.

depicts work as a necessary and wholesome part of human life rather than as punishment.

There is great significance in the biblical account of man and woman being made in the image of God, who himself worked six days creating the heavens and the earth, not resting until the seventh day. It is also significant that the biblical account goes on to tell how Adam was put in the garden of Eden "to till it and keep it" *before* he disobeyed God and was driven from the garden. Adam's punishment after his disobedience was not that he should continue to work; it lay, rather, in the fact that the ground he tilled would grow "thorns and thistles" until human work, like human love, could be reborn and made bright and new, again and again.

A word of warning may be in order before leaving the subject of theology and pastoral counseling in work crises. There are wide variations in the needs of particular human beings, variations which are sometimes obscured by the broad brush of theological generalities. David Riesman provides this word of warning regarding the need to work, at least in the case of the healthy aging whose vocational identity may be lost or threatened.[2] He finds the aging acting in not one but three different behavioral patterns. Riesman cites a relatively small proportion of the aging whose inner resources free them from the limitations the culture places on the aging. These he calls the "autonomous." He describes the majority of the elderly as the "adjusted" because they depend on work, power, and any other supports which may be available in the culture to keep them going. In his third category he places the aging who lack both inner and exterior protection—the "anomic" who simply decay. Of such a person Riesman said: "He held a job less than the job held him. . . . Such people live like cards, propped up by other cards."[3]

---

[2] The healthy aging in this study are considered as not having reached Erikson's last developmental crisis. Although they may be of the same age as those in his final stage, the healthy aging have not yet experienced "the decline of bodily and mental functions" he ascribes to those in his eighth stage (Erik H. Erikson, *Insight and Responsibility* [New York: W. W. Norton & Co., Inc., 1964], p. 133; and *Childhood and Society*, 2nd ed. [New York: W. W. Norton & Co., Inc., 1963], p. 274). Nor do they yet need to face the despair that threatens when "time is . . . too short for the attempt to start another life and to try out alternate roads to integrity" (Erikson, *Childhood and Society*, p. 269).

[3] David Riesman, *Selected Essays from Individualism Reconsidered* (Garden City, N.Y.: Doubleday Anchor Books, imprint of Doubleday & Company, Inc., 1954), pp. 164, 165, 167, 172. Good use is made of Reisman's theory by Rosalie H. Roseñfeld in her article, "The Elderly Mystique." *Journal of Social Issues,* vol. 21, no. 4 (October, 1965), p. 42.

THE INCREASING NEED FOR COUNSELING IN WORK CRISES

Reference was made in the introductory chapter of this book to the rapidly increasing number of work crises in our society among healthy persons of all ages. There is no way to compute the number accurately; even those who are acutely dissatisfied with their jobs are still listed as employed. Statistics and figures of all kinds are available, however, which clearly suggest the magnitude of the problem.

It is possible, for instance, to approximate the number of healthy persons over sixty-five. They constitute a substantial segment of the healthy aging; and with both compulsory and voluntary retirement of men and women over sixty-five becoming more common, they are becoming more and more susceptible to work crises. If only a small proportion of the healthy aging were in work crises and needed and sought counseling, their number would be awesome. According to most estimates, 80 percent of all persons over sixty-five are healthy; only 10 percent of them are classified as sick or senile, the remaining 10 percent are infirm or housebound. The following report also leaves no doubt that the number of people over sixty-five and their proportion to the total population will be rapidly increasing:

> The proportion of elderly in the U.S. population has also been changing throughout the century. In 1900 about 4 percent of the nation's 76 million people were 65 years old or over. Forty years later, although their numbers had tripled, they were still only 5.4 percent of the total population. By 1970, however, about one out of 10 Americans (9.9 percent) were elderly.
>
> No matter which fertility projection proves valid, the proportion of the aged will increase between 2010 and 2020 as the baby-boom cohort of the late 1940's and the early 1950's reaches senior citizen status. It can be reasonably expected that the 40 million elderly of the year 2020 will be 13 to 15 percent of U.S. population.[4]

At the other end of the age spectrum, among young people in work crises because they are facing the job market for the first time, the need for counseling and guidance is beginning to be widely recognized. On November 16, 1976, the *New York Times* published a special section, Section 11, entitled "Fall Survey of Education and Career Development." On the first page of that section Frank J. Prial wrote this in a lead article:

[4]"The Elderly in America" in *Population Bulletin* (Washington, D.C.: Population Reference Bureau, Inc., 1975), vol. 30, no. 3, pp. 5-7.

Career guidance and job-hunting, like . . . clean clothes, seem to be enjoying renewed importance and prestige on campuses around the country.

At dozens of colleges and universities, students are actually getting academic credit for learning how to find a job. And schools not yet tuned in to the latest innovations in career guidance are paying a new breed of consultant thousands of dollars to show them what to do.[5]

The significance of entering into a mature work relationship after school or college has been mentioned in the third section of the preceding chapter. A job, along with a mature love relationship, gives one an identity which marks the resolution of the crisis of adolescence and young adulthood. Important as this finding of the first real job is, however, this event does not mark the end of the work crises that may still lie ahead for most people before they face retirement. Richard N. Bolles, who is prominent in the field of career guidance, on the first page of his Preface to *What Color Is Your Parachute?* has this to say about that long interim period:

And how many times will you have to go about the job-hunt? Who can say, in your particular case? But you may be interested to know that according to experts, the average worker under thirty-five years of age goes about the job-hunt once every one-and-half years! And the average worker over thirty-five, once every three years![6]

One index of the increasing number of people who need and do seek counseling in work crises is the astonishing growth of what the *New York Times* article, cited earlier in this section, calls "a new breed of consultant," namely, the career guidance counselor. In *What Color Is Your Parachute?* Bolles has prepared an appendix containing a substantial directory of professional help available to those in work crises, listed under the headings: "Help for Anyone," "Help for Those Who Are Unemployed," "Help for Women," "Help for Clergy and Religious," and "Help for Those Who Conclude They Want to Deal with Their Interior Furniture";[7] and this follows another appendix which lists and describes a substantial number of books available for self-help in work crises. One is left to conclude that the need for counseling in work crises is increasing at least in

[5] Frank J. Prial, "Fall Survey of Education and Career Development," *New York Times*, November 16, 1976, Section 11, p. 1.

[6] Richard N. Bolles, *What Color Is Your Parachute?* (Berkeley, Calif.: Ten Speed Press, 1977).

[7] *Ibid.*, pp. 202-226.

proportion to the ever increasing number of people in these crises.

Many of the work crises prior to normal retirement age are "accidental" in the sense that they are caused by loss of a job, ill health, or other factors which cannot be anticipated. Erikson identified one crisis that *can* be anticipated is midlife; therefore, he included the crisis of "maturity" in his eight "developmental" crises and suggests that it can affect the work and the love relationships of the persons involved in the crisis. The crisis of midlife appears when either a psychic change or an external event causes a man or a women to look ahead into the future and say with Hamlet:

> How weary, stale, flat, and unprofitable
> Seem to me all the uses of this world![8]

It is at this point, Erikson maintains, that a person in one's thirties or forties faces a fork in the road. One way is progressive and leads to "generativity," which he defines as primarily a widening care and concern for establishing and guiding the next generation as parent, mentor, or teacher; the other way he sees as regressive, because it leads to the stagnation and boredom produced by a narrowing adherence to an irreversible obligation or by a narrowing concern for oneself.[9]

It remained for Gail Sheehy, in 1974, to bring to wide public notice the midlife developmental crisis in work relationships, and often in love relationships, that Erikson had identified in 1950. She did this in her extraordinarily popular book, *Passages.* Early in the book, Sheehy explained that she had substituted the word "passages" for "crises" because she felt it was a less confusing and "less loaded word for the critical transitions between [life] stages."[10] In *Passages* she concentrated on the transition of midlife, and she used as data the case histories of a great number of living men and women whom she had interviewed.

Sheehy's case histories have given me a delayed understanding of my own midlife career change, as well as those of friends and former parishioners. Like many others who served for several years in World

---

[8] *Hamlet,* act 1, scene 2, lines 133-134.
[9] Erikson, *Childhood and Society,* pp. 266, 267. Erikson did not dwell on this crisis because, as he noted on page 266: "In this book the emphasis is on the childhood stages, otherwise the section on generativity would of necessity be the central one. . . ." A few years later he did write *Young Man Luther,* his monumental case study of the identity crisis of Martin Luther's young manhood.
[10] Gail Sheehy, *Passages* (New York: E. P. Dutton, 1974), p. 19.

War II, I had to decide in my late thirties whether or not to go back to my former work when I was discharged. (It had not been difficult for me to decline a permanent commission in the armed services.) I had enjoyed practicing law in my hometown, the county seat of an agricultural community. At the same time I had also received great satisfaction from my activities as a Sunday school teacher, lay reader, and vestryman in my local parish church, as well as from my activities in the diocese and national church. Although I was married, my wife and I had only one infant child; I also had the resources, with added government assistance, to get the seminary education needed for the ordained ministry. My decision was to go for the ordained ministry, which seemed to me to offer a wider field for care and concern than did my former career; in addition, it did not offer the same prospect of possible "stagnation and boredom" (Erikson's terms) as did life in my hometown.

More absorbing than my own case, as I think about it today, was the opportunity I missed to counsel my dear friend, Bob. Bob was a few years older, but we had grown up in the same community, practiced law contemporaneously, been active together in the same parish church, and had similar military service. Bob, who had three children approaching their teens and no outside income, had returned to his law practice when I told him of my decision to enter the ministry. Bob's only comment was to reply: "I think I envy you more than any man I know."

The opportunity I missed was to remind my friend that he, while practicing law, had been a Christian pastor to more people in that community than any ordained minister there—which had been true, regardless of whether those he counseled were clients or not. Perhaps Bob could have been helped to see that his return to the law, which was necessary financially, did not mean for him regression to a narrowing obligation. Unfortunately, Bob was killed shortly afterwards when his automobile was struck by the drunken driver of another car.

At least one crisis of maturity has received a wryly humorous exposition. The following press release of Representative Otis G. Pike (Democrat of New York) appeared in *The Washington Post,* page 1, February 11, 1978. The article prefaces the following statement with the phrase, "Said Pike of Pike":

"He's been a public servant 25 years, a congressman 18. He feels good. He could get reelected. He wants a different career. His motivation is slipping. People bug him. He has no privacy. He doesn't like campaigning. He doesn't like fund raising.

"The wisdom of the ages has not been secretly entrusted solely to Democrats. Both parties are indifferent to the national debt, the deficit or any obligation to pay our bills or balance our budget.

"He's tired of wasting his time on drivel. He'll get a good pension. He'll miss it, but can learn to make his own plane reservations and balance his own checkbook.

"A transcript of (this) entire 14-minute soporific is available in the congressman's office. The office is closed today." [11]

There is no way to compute the number of people in work crises between adolescence and retirement or the number of the healthy aging who are in work crises after retirement. It follows that one cannot say how many of them might need and seek some kind of counseling if it were readily available to them. It can be said that their number is rapidly increasing.

THE PASTOR'S UNIQUE OPPORTUNITY AS COUNSELOR IN WORK CRISES

The pastor, in his usual role as minister to a congregation, is rarely turned to in work crises. This is evident when one compares this with the frequency with which people have traditionally turned to the pastor in crises involving their love relationships. One reason for not calling on him for help in work crises may be a general awareness of the decided difference in the career system that engages the pastor and the systems which engage those to whom he ministers. [12] In another connection Bolles makes much of the fact that clergy, along with the military, "have been members of a closed social system, somewhat isolated from the mainstream of society, in which roles and status positions were defined, paternalism was encouraged, and security was promised." [13] The average lay person might well question what a pastor could know about a work crisis.

Any reluctance to seek pastoral counseling in work crises is unfortunate for several reasons. Pastors are, among other things, readily available at little or no cost, and people know the way to their

[11] "Reps. Pike and Waggonner Announce They Are Retiring," *The Washington Post*, February 11, 1978, p. 1.

[12] In many dioceses of the Protestant Episcopal Church in the U.S.A., there is a policy not to ordain qualified ministerial candidates for whom there are no positions waiting. Because ordination confers on clergy a professional standing similar in many respects to that of lawyers, the diocesan policy referred to stands in sharp contrast to the practice of licensing all lawyers who have passed their bar examinations.

[13] Bolles, *op. cit.*, p. 222.

doors. Howard J. Clinebell, Jr., presents convincing documentation for his observations on this subject: "There is no doubt that *ministers occupy a central and strategic role as counselors in our society.* It is obvious that clergymen are on the front lines in the struggle to lift the loads of troubled persons!"[14]

In addition to availability, custom, and financial cost, there is often another incentive for turning first to the pastor when there is a chance one may be facing a work crisis. A person may chat informally with a pastor at the church door, on the street, or elsewhere without admitting that a problem of any kind exists. Such informal conversations give one an opportunity first to sound out the pastor and then decide whether or not to admit one's fears or doubts. If the decision is "yes" and the possibility of a problem is mutually recognized, arrangements can be made to discuss it in detail. Should it then develop that there is, in fact, a problem, the advice and support of the pastor is available whether the pastor continues as counselor or makes a referral to a specialist.

Contrast this with the circumstance of a person first taking the initiative to call a career guidance counselor or a psychiatrist or a lawyer. The same fears and doubts are present, but there is often a forbidding hurdle involved in the lonely decision to admit their existence to oneself, to the specialized counselor, and (one sometimes suspects) to the world.

There are also distinctive opportunities for the *pastor* to take the initiative for counseling in work crises. It would be highly unprofessional for a career guidance counselor to do so, as it would be for any other specialized counselor. But this is not true for the pastor! A Christian minister may be called upon by a congregation (or, for job counseling, by a member of it) to serve it when it requests; a Christian minister, however, also has another call—the call from God. The minister is, among other things, an *apostle,* "sent" by God, to serve him by serving the congregation. This is the source of the pastor's initiative. This initiative is exercised in preaching, teaching, and leading in worship. It is also properly exercised in pastoral relationships. Of course, the practice of this initiative requires sensitivity to the needs and feelings of those to be served, but this

---

[14] Howard J. Clinebell, Jr., *Basic Types of Pastoral Counseling* (Nashville: Abingdon Press, 1966), p. 43. Clinebell's presented documentation comes from Gerald Gurin, Joseph Veroff, and Sheila Field, *Americans View Their Mental Health* (New York: Basic Books, Inc., Publishers, 1960).

sensitivity is no different from that required in preaching, teaching, or leading worship.

An example of pastoral initiative in counseling may be found in the first case study, involving George, in chapter 2. In the course of a casual conversation Canon Wedel probed deeply into George's work relationship, raised the issue of his quitting the job, and even suggested that continuing with it might be fatal! On the other hand, George's ongoing "pastor" continued to do nothing but manifest a concern for his Christian education. Surely one reason I feel strongly about pastoral initiative in work crises is my failure to take any such initiative with George, although there were many occasions to do so after I became aware of the crisis.

Preaching and teaching are the pastor's ongoing opportunities to confront the entire congregation with the widespread existence for work crises. They are also opportunities for exposure of the pastor's concern and availability for counseling in this crucial area. After they have been brought out in the open and had their stigma removed, work crises can then be accessible not only to the pastor, but also to all Christian people who seek to follow Paul's injunction to "bear one another's burdens."

Much has been said already about the variety of work crises in our society. The work crisis most commonly faced, because it is "developmental" and therefore inevitable (in Erikson's terms), is the work crisis of late adolescence or young adulthood. In creating and utilizing a pastor's unusual opportunities to counsel young people, the pastor can fulfill many of the functions of "mentor."

The mentor's role is ancient and honorable and not to be covered in a few words here. Yet, it might not violate the concept of "mentor" to suggest that pastors share one attribute with mentors: the pastor can serve as a mentor in that he or she does not have with the young person the paternal or maternal connection which usually disqualifies parents, so often a part of the problem, from serving as mentors. The need for mentors is particularly acute today when families are so often on the move. This mobility causes uncles, aunts, and old family friends—who in the past often served as mentors without the title—to be unavailable to the present younger generation. If there were no other reason for women in the pastorate, the opportunity to serve young women as counselors - mentors would justify their ordination.

Pastors of both sexes are needed if they are, like Martin Luther's classic mentor, Staupitz, to fulfill the mentor's indispensable purposes: first, understanding and identifying with the problems of young adult men and women, and then putting them to work.[15]

The role of mentor is particularly appropriate for unordained or ordained pastors in midlife, whose care and concern for the next generation goes beyond any children they might have. An example of such a lay mentor was my father. In my family there were also two daughters, one two years older and the other two years younger than I. Our home was a gathering place for our contemporaries of both sexes, partly because our father was for years a good mentor to our friends. He first taught us all as young children to swim in ponds and then in the Mississippi River. There were no swimming pools or formal instruction available, and he wanted us to be prepared, as he had not been, before we went swimming on our own. Then, before we hurt one another by carelessly using air rifles, he taught us to use a .22 caliber rifle, which we respected. When we reached high school age, he taught us in a Sunday school Bible class, where we developed an intelligent love and respect for the Bible. In his own words, he wanted to prepare us "for our first college bull sessions." He knew that we might be left with no real faith if we went away with only the fundamentalist approach to the Bible that was generally taught the young in that part of the South at that time. Later on, he would give us rudimentary career guidance by urging us to look at alternative job openings rather than simply to accept the first one that came along, just as he had taught us to play bridge as an alternative to "shooting dice." He would remind us that we were too smart to marry the first person of the opposite sex who was willing to marry us; and then he would go on to say that we would probably spend more waking hours with our jobs than we would with our spouses.

This "mentoring" all took place at least fifty years ago; and it was a community where an able physician, such as my father, could have the respect of not just the young, but their parents and grandparents as well. It would be difficult to duplicate that situation in today's mobile society. On the other hand, the intervening fifty years have seen the development of youth work by ordained and unordained pastors in congregations and communities, along with camps and conference centers. Equivalent opportunities are here for today's mentors to progress through maturity as they guide a rootless younger generation that sorely needs such care and concern.

[15] Erik H. Erikson, *Young Man Luther* (New York: W. W. Norton & Co., Inc., 1962), p. 165.

4

Equipping the Pastor for Counseling in Work Crises

THE FIRST STEP: ACKNOWLEDGING THE PASTOR'S OWN WORK CRISES

The purpose of this book, as stated in the introductory chapter, is not "to make pastors experts in the field of career guidance"; it is designed, rather, "to foster a climate of opinion that will encourage ordained and lay pastors to recognize the existence of work crises throughout their congregations." It is my conviction that once the need for pastoral counseling in these crises is recognized, both ordained and unordained pastors will equip themselves to meet the counseling needs of the people they serve.

The Introduction also contains the statement that "pastors are a conscientious lot." It is no contradiction to add that they are also a very human lot. This means that pastors share a limitation that our common humanity imposes on even the most conscientious; that is, it is very difficult to minister to the pain of others when there is not at least an echo of a similar pain in the person who would be the minister. Pastors who are not conscious of any past or present work crises are not eliminated thereby from ministering to others in such crises. For there still remains an impending work crisis facing all pastors who are willing to look at it: retirement. Clear thinking about retirement can precipitate a healthy concern about this work crisis relatively early in one's professional life. To use a personal example, it was the mere thinking about my own retirement and how best to prepare for it that led me to my consideration of work crises in general.

In *Romeo and Juliet* (act II, scene 2, line 1) Romeo's young friends have been making fun of his love for Juliet. Shakespeare puts into his mouth the classic response: "He jests at scars that never felt a wound." This is by no means intended to suggest that pastors who have not recognized their own past, present, or impending work crises jest at the work crises of others; it is only intended to emphasize a kind of human insensitivity to needs that are as yet unrecognized in oneself.

The word "unrecognized" is used advisedly with regard to pastors' own work crises. For almost a generation every thoughtful research project of which I am aware regarding the practice of ministry has documented work crises of one kind or another that are shared by an overwhelming percentage of clergy. In 1957 Training for Ministry, a confidential research project, was carried out by the Russell Sage Foundation in cooperation with five seminaries from as many Protestant denominations. This survey broke ground in its revelation of widespread clergy dissatisfaction. Under way since 1973 is a very extensive research project, Readiness for Ministry, being conducted by the Association of Theological Schools in the United States and Canada with funding from the Lilly Endowment, Inc. Two books already produced by the Association's project, *Criteria* and *Assessment,*[1] document the painful stresses and ambiguities that can be anticipated in the practice of ministry.

It is with the best intentions that clergy often hesitate to recognize their own work crises. One reason is that such recognition might be interpreted as evidence that they had been mistaken about their call to serve God's people in the ordained ministry. This interpretation of job dissatisfaction has led many able and devoted clergy to leave the ordained ministry. That was the finding of at least one denominational survey in 1970:

> Despite the fact that the minister occupies a position of esteem and status, discontent and dissatisfaction among clergymen have become pronounced. Dissatisfaction has reached the point where significant

[1] *Criteria* (Vandalia, Ohio: Association of Theological Schools, 1975) and *Assessment* (Vandalia, Ohio: Association of Theological Schools, 1976).

numbers of men in many denominations have left the parish ministry to pursue careers in other fields.[2]

Another reason for the hesitancy of clergy to recognize their own work crises is the idea that suffering should be expected by one who has elected to follow Christ, "the Suffering Servant of God," in the ordained ministry. There are several difficulties with this attitude. One is a mistaken kind of clerical "elitism" in the field of suffering, for it is not at ordination, but at the baptism of Christians, where one takes on the life, death, and resurrection of Christ. Another difficulty with the general acceptance of suffering is that it fails to differentiate needless suffering from the suffering which obedience to the will of God can bring. The latter is ultimately transformed into joy in the Christian story. Time and time again, however, the pain of work crises falls in the category of needless suffering; and the failure to admit this pain and to do something about it can be as misguided as the failure to admit the existence of a rock in one's shoe.

There is still a third reason why clergy may fail to recognize their own work crises: this is the haunting fear that nothing can be done about them. There are all kinds of stories going around, some of them accurate, about the supply of clergy exceeding the demand for them in many denominations. So, one might conclude, why worry oneself, one's family, the governing board of the congregation or denominational officials with futile complaints? Meanwhile there are bills to be paid and children to educate. In cases like this, the accepted plan too often seems to be just to shut one's eyes to the problem, pretend it does not exist, and maybe, *maybe,* it will go away.

There is a kind of irony in the failure of clergy to acknowledge openly their own past, present, or impending work crises, whether anything can be done about them or not. Stoicism on the part of Christian clergy and lay leaders is not only unbecoming; it also cuts them off from those to whom they would minister. This thesis was clearly stated and documented in *Assessment,* volume 2, of the Association of Theological Schools' Readiness for Ministry project. On page 8 the editors have this to say:

> Our day has become wary of the glib answer. People have been disappointed too many times; they have followed too many who would sell packaged hope. None of the painless solutions worked. They listen

[2]"Who Do Men Say That I Am?" A Report on Identity and the Parish Priest in the Episcopal Church, p. 1, published by the Executive Council of the Episcopal Church, 815 Second Ave., New York, N.Y., September 24, 1970.

no longer to suggestions shouted from the sidelines. Only the one who has experienced the pain, the frustrations, the struggle of living fully in a moment such as ours—and has both glimpsed meaning and has personally heard the word of hope—dares speak to us. Only those who have been wounded may speak of healing. Only those who have come to grips with their own loneliness are able to enter into the loneliness of another. This is not to romanticize the pain of ambiguity or loneliness; it is not an encouragement for a superficial swapping of stories of personal distress. It affirms the answer pastorally fashioned by Henri Nouwen (author of *The Wounded Healer: Ministry in Contemporary Society* [New York: Doubleday & Co., 1972]) of the minister as the one who acknowledges his own humanity and uses this awareness as a vehicle of ministry.[3]

THE SECOND STEP: CAREER GUIDANCE AND PLANNING FOR PASTORS THEMSELVES

The premise of this entire chapter is that once ordained or lay pastors acknowledge their own work crises and know that help is available, they will go to work on the crises with a two-fold purpose: to help themselves and to equip themselves to help others in their congregations who are also in work crises. While there was little competent help available in this area a few years ago, able professional assistance and materials for self-help are very accessible today. Financial aid for professional help is also to be had in many judicatories.

In the late 1960s several denominations quickly got the message of clergy dissatisfaction which was signaled by such surveys as those referred to in the preceding section. Denominational officials realized the importance of making help available to clergy and lay leaders in these crises. There were already individual career guidance counselors who had been doing notable work for a number of years. Bernard Haldane, a leading practitioner and author in the field today, had begun in 1945 counseling with returning World War II veterans seeking career guidance for civilian life. He and others like him were available to help in setting up official career development centers for clergy and lay leaders. The centers now number fifteen, widely scattered across the country, and all are accredited and coordinated by the Career Development Council, 475 Riverside Drive, New York City. The centers are listed in *What Color Is Your Parachute?* pages 219-221.

As a preface to his listing the author has this to say about "Help

[3] *Assessment* (Vandalia, Ohio; Association of Theological Schools, 1976), p. 8.

for Clergy and Religious": "Probably no profession has developed, or had developed for it, so many resources to aid in career assessment as has the clerical profession."[4] He then goes on to warn of the differences in the offerings of various counseling services, differences that should be explored before any commitment to them is made. Some, for example, limit their services to career *assessment,* that is, assisting counselees in identifying their skills and aptitudes, particularly those which they get the most satisfaction out of using. Bolles recommends, instead, counselors who offer career *development.* Career "development" includes an assessment of *what* skills and aptitudes a person might have and enjoy using; however, career development counseling goes on to include assistance in determining *where* these skills might best be employed—on the present job under different conditions or on another job in a different work environment; and, finally, career development includes coaching as to *how* one might go about effecting the necessary changes in the conditions of the present job or locating new work in a more satisfactory environment where the same skills would be valued.

The centers recognized by the Career Development Council constitute just one route which pastors can follow for professional help with their own work crises. There are also the seminaries which, like denominations, now recognize the need for career guidance and planning. As a result, courses in career development are now being included in the curricula of many Continuing Education and Doctor of Divinity programs. Students preparing for the ministry are also being encouraged more and more to accept the discipline of the same reflection and guidance to help them personally in present and future work crises, as well as to equip them to counsel others to whom they will be ministering.

Dean Harvey H. Guthrie, Jr., of the Episcopal Divinity School in Cambridge, Massachusetts, had this to say about career planning in seminary in the spring, 1977, issue of *EDS News:*

> In a new situation in which ministry cannot be equated with "making a living," in which our graduates are not automatically taken care of (as we were when I graduated) by the church, a seminary has to take responsibility for equipping its graduates for finding what their ministries should be, for finding where the money is to come from. We have not had to do that before. It has been taken care of by "the system."

---

[4] Richard N. Bolles, *What Color Is Your Parachute?* (Berkeley, Calif.: Ten Speed Press, 1977), p. 219.

"Placement" and "career development" have not been explicitly on the docket of Episcopal seminaries.

But we now have that responsibility. Coping with job seeking, with trying to get vocation to square with what one is paid for, with "career planning" as part of ministry, had better become intentional. I believe they can become intentional without violating the sound virtue of humility in its proper sense. That is why this spring we are offering a series of workshops on career planning for seniors and others interested. We have engaged an MTS graduate, Peter Stapleton, and a former trial fellow student, Constance Buchanan, to spend two four-hour sessions and then further small group and individual sessions with those who have signed on.

The nature of our mission today and for the future is such that more time and thought are going to have to be spent on that. We need to think about building that into the curriculum. We are here to equip Christians for ministry, and helping them in this new situation to take responsibility for their own—as one book puts it—intentional ministries is a part of our task.[5]

The secular individuals, agencies, and organizations where career guidance is available are too numerous to count, much less to evaluate.[6] Some, such as state university systems and community colleges, have residency requirements; others are open to all comers. Some require personal attendance; others operate by mail. The point is that they are many and varied, lasting from one day to one semester. Bolles, in the listings referred to above, includes 135 agencies and organizations, mostly colleges and universities, where career guidance is available *just for women.* He admits that even this list is not exhaustive, nor does he make any recommendations.

Although professional help is at hand for ordained and lay pastors in a great many ways, there are many pastors who may find it more convenient or suitable to go the "do-it-yourself" route. Many of the professionals in the field have realized this and written books that can be used for this purpose by individuals or groups. In 1960, Bernard Haldane, that pioneer in the field of career counseling, published *How to Make a Habit of Success.* He republished this classic in a revised, paperback edition and wrote another helpful book, *Career Satisfaction and Success: A Guide to Job Freedom.*[7]

[5] *EDS News,* Spring, 1977, p. 6.

[6] Bolles also has good advice with regard to evaluation of career guidance counselors and agencies in Bolles, *op. cit.,* pp. 49-53.

[7] Bernard Haldane, *How to Make a Habit of Success,* rev. ed. (Washington, D.C.: Acropolis Books, 1975); and Haldane, *Career Satisfaction and Success: A Guide to Job Freedom,* ed. William Olcheski (New York: AMACOM, a division of American Management Associations, 1974).

References have already been made to *What Color Is Your Parachute?* by Richard N. Bolles, who is an ordained Episcopal minister and Director of the National Career Development Project of United Ministries in Higher Education, an ecumenical endeavor. Bolles's book is a good starting book, as it is not limited to any particular work crisis. Its bibliography and other appendices, suggesting specialized books and other resources, are updated in a new edition every year.

There are two related difficulties in any "do-it-yourself" method of career guidance. The first is that it is very lonely work, and the second is the universal temptation to procrastinate. Both difficulties can be obviated if one has a partner or two in the process or assembles a group of like-minded persons. The partner could be a spouse, a colleague, or any friend who shares the same interest. A group could very well be assembled from a congregation or a local clergy association.

Partners and group members can do more than provide companionship and help in maintaining a disciplined schedule. Their presence is especially valuable in exercises involving skill assessment, for example. Two or three acquaintances doing these exercises together can counterbalance the kind of self-effacing modesty that our culture tends to induce. A solitary individual assessing personal skills tends to disclaim some of those already exhibited. There are very few who do not need someone else to say, "Of course you can do that! Remember when you. . . ?" In this way pastors can begin counseling others even while they are equipping themselves for the crisis counseling ministry.

THE THIRD STEP: HELPING OTHERS IN WORK CRISES

There are basically two ways a pastor can help people in work crises:

1. The pastor can help them find jobs. This is the route the employment agencies take; while the agency may be successful, the statistics clearly indicate that the job seeker usually stays only a short time on a job which is found in this manner.

2. The pastor can help them learn a *process* that will (*a*) give them information about themselves, their skills, and their priorities, and (*b*) give information about where and how to look for satisfying work. Richard N. Bolles has described this

way as teaching one to fish rather than simply giving the person a fish.[8]

This section on "Helping Others in Work Crises" was intentionally preceded by the section on "Career Guidance and Planning for Pastors Themselves." The reason for this ordering of material is that learning how to fish oneself is the best preparation for teaching others to fish. Rather than dismiss the subject with such a platitude, however, concrete questions and answers by Bolles are set out in an article in the December, 1977, issue of *Newsletter,* a regular publication of the National Career Development Project:

> In the back of each copy of *Parachute* you have a HOTLINE page that the reader can send to the National Career Development Project's (NCDP) headquarters. When readers send this in, what is the most common question they ask?
>
> The most common question asked is for the information regarding a particular place to go, in looking for a job. For example, a reader will say, "I am interested in doing career development for a private industry having an in-house training program. Please send me a list of such industries and businesses."
>
> Do you maintain such lists?
> No, but even if we did, we wouldn't send them to the readers requesting them.
>
> Why is that?
> Our goal, here at the NCDP, is not merely to render services to job hunters and career changers, but to empower them. We do not want merely to rescue them from their present dire predicament, but to teach them a process which they can use as long as they live. It is therefore more important, from our point of view, that they learn how to go about finding out information for themselves, rather than having that information simply served up to them this one particular time.
>
> Well, how would you teach someone to go about finding out information for themselves?
> Essentially it involves using their contacts to find one person

---

[8] In fairness to the state employment agencies, it should be stated that they usually provide job counselors who will do some preliminary work with job seekers free of charge, if such counseling is requested.

who is doing the sort of thing they are looking for. That person, then, will lead them to others, who will lead them to others, who will lead them to others, etc. For example, the person or job-hunter who is interested in doing career development for a private industry having an in-house training program needs to ask all of his or her acquaintances: What business or industry here (or in my chosen geographical preference) has such a program, and who is in charge of it?

Can you give other examples?

Sure. If you are interested in putting together two careers that you have never heard of being combined before, ask all of your acquaintances (i.e., contacts) who they know that is in either of those careers. Then go to that person, and ask him or her who they know that has combined both.

If you are interested in doing a particular kind of work without getting the sort of training or credential that most people in that sort of work believe they have to have, ask all your acquaintances for the name of someone who is in that kind of work. Then, go ask them who they know that got into this work without the proper training or credential.

If you are interested in starting a store that sells homemade candles and soap, go to all your acquaintances (that includes your friendly neighborhood librarian and your chamber of commerce) to ask them who is already in a similar business.

It seems to me, in a nutshell, that you are saying, go talk to somebody who is already doing the sort of thing you are interested in doing.

Exactly. And that your contacts, broadly defined, are the best way of finding such people.

What is the next most common question you get asked in the HOTLINE?

We get asked, what kind of work should a person with my skills (and here they list the skills they have identified) go into?

Have they usually identified their skills correctly?

Yes, but they haven't prioritized them—to say which ones are most important to them and which ones are least important to them. Once they've done that—we usually refer them to the prioritizing device in Appendix E of *Where Do I Go from Here with My Life?*—they can then go about finding out information about the sort of jobs that would use those skills, by doing the information search we referred to above.[9]

Congruent with Bolles's approach to assistance in career search is the approach of the new Office of Career Services and Off-Campus Learning at Harvard College. The January, 1978, issue of *Forum,* published by the Harvard College Fund, succinctly states the purpose of their career services:

> . . . . Students who have learned how to identify career objectives and how to conduct a search leading to their fulfillment can, says Ginn [Director of the Office], "provide themselves with career advice at any age and in any place."[10]

A pastor who is counseling someone in a work crisis may choose to recommend one or more of the routes suggested earlier for the pastor himself. Among those routes the pastor might recommend would be:

1. Professional services which include career development as well as career assessment;
2. The "do-it-yourself" route, making use of the books and exercises available for individuals and groups;
3. The "do-it-with-others" route recommended earlier for clergy.

One route not mentioned earlier could be to refer the counselee to a lay support group in the congregation or community. It should not be too difficult for the pastor to enlist a support group of concerned lay persons who have successfully passed through work crises which had much in common with the counselee's present crisis. They could be of great help to many in work crises; they themselves might also welcome the opportunity for such a creative lay ministry.[11]

---

[9] Richard N. Bolles, "Answers to Questions We Often Get Asked," in *Newsletter* (Walnut Hill, Calif.: National Career Development Project), December, 1977, pp. 1, 4.

[10] *Forum,* January, 1978.

[11] For more on individual and group lay ministry see chapter 11, "The Layman's Ministry of Pastoral Care and Counseling," in Howard J. Clinebell, Jr., *Basic Types of Pastoral Counseling* (Nashville: Abingdon Press, 1966), pp. 282-293.

5

A General Methodology
for Counseling in
Work Crises

THE USE OF METHODOLOGY

> Every step has its sound,
> Every road has its song,
> When you know where you are going
> And why.
> > "Israeli Marching Song"[1]

[Alice] went on. "Would you tell me, please, which way I ought to go from here?"

"That depends a good deal on where you want to get to," said the Cat.

"I don't much care where—," said Alice.

"Then it doesn't matter which way you go," said the Cat.[2]

Christian pastors who seek to help others in work crises, unlike Alice, know *"where* they want to go." They want to share a part of our Lord's mission, and so they want to go to those to whom they minister with the kind of help that will enable them to have life "more abundantly," to have life "in all its fullness" (see John 10:10, KJV and NEB, respectively).

---

[1]Quoted by Jo Rachel Backer in an address at Princeton University, printed in *Princeton Alumni Weekly*, March 11, 1975, p. 4.

[2]Lewis Carroll, *Alice's Adventures in Wonderland, Through the Looking Glass,* and *The Hunting of the Snark* (New York: The Modern Library, n.d.), p. 86.

Pastors are more like the Israeli marchers. They also know *why* they seek this end. They want to share the love of God they have known in Christ and in the children of God in whom his Spirit moves on earth.

However, the best incentive and the best motivation are "necessary but not sufficient" (to borrow Reinhold Niebuhr's distinction); they are not sufficient for pastoral counseling in general or for work crises counseling in particular. The most conscientious pastor can know *where* and *why* and still share Alice's quandary as to which *way* to go to get there or *how* to accomplish the mission once there. Answers to questions like *"Which way* ought I to go?" or *"How* do I do it?"* are the stuff of methodology. Pastoral career guidance counseling, like any specific branch of knowledge, has its methodology, i.e., a system of principles, practices, and procedures.

This does not mean that counseling where work relationships are involved has a *unique* methodology. An attempt was made in earlier chapters to point out the great similarity between counseling in work crises and counseling in crises where love relationships are involved. There are also general principles applicable to all pastoral counseling.

Three such general principles are identified by Howard J. Clinebell, Jr., in chapter 4 of *Basic Types of Pastoral Counseling*. They are "establishing rapport, disciplined listening, responding to feelings." Later in the book, when discussing educative counseling, Clinebell has this to say:

> To discover what may be relevant to a person's needs requires listening and interacting with a person. It requires becoming aware of his internal and external (interpersonal) frames of reference. To distribute information and advice in counseling, prior to understanding the person's situation, weakens the counselee's trust in the counselor. Ideally, the teaching aspects of counseling should be focused as sharply on the person's particular needs as is the medicine which a competent physician gives for a specific malady.[3]

Establishing Rapport

There are few pastors who would not like to forget instances in which they prescribed remedies for maladies before listening to learn whether those maladies actually existed. I, for example, was having a serious conversation with an old friend while bubbling over with my recent discovery of Erik Erikson's stress on the importance of work

---

[3] Howard J. Clinebell, Jr., *Basic Types of Pastoral Counseling* (Nashville: Abingdon Press, 1966), p. 191.

relationships. The friend had recently retired after long tenure in a most demanding job that had been, in the last few years especially, very difficult to carry out. After being told by me as his volunteer pastor that he should get on another horse promptly and go back to work, the friend gently replied: "Look, I am bone-tired; I have no financial or emotional need to go back to work; and I have no idea of doing it, certainly not in the foreseeable future." Fortunately, our friendship survived the incident.

Essentially the same general principles which Clinebell identifies regarding pastoral counseling were spotted by Theodore O. Wedel, although Wedel was writing specifically of a strategy for mission. In *The Gospel in a Strange, New World* he wrote in his winsome way:

> French evangelistic literature has brought to the fore three words that summarize by way of three successive steps the church's mission strategy. The three words are: *présence, service, communication* (give them the honor of French pronunciation, and they escape the handicap of shopworn familiarity). Incarnational evangelism is first of all the *présence* of the church in the world. Though not much has been said in this exposition of *service* (*diakonia,* or "deaconing"), presence and service are intimately related. Communication, however, must wait until its hour has come. Witness to the gospel must win the right to be heard.[4]

Listening

When teaching, Wedel sometimes illustrated the application of the same three steps to pastoral counseling with a story of a friend of his, Dr. John Doe:

Dr. Doe was rector of a substantial parish in a large metropolitan community. A man he knew only by name had made an hour's appointment with him through the parish secretary. At the appointed time the man came to Dr. Doe's study, and the two of them said, "How do you do," shook hands and sat down. Dr. Doe waited for the man to bring up the matter he had on his mind. He waited two minutes, five minutes, ten minutes. (In describing his experience Dr. Doe said that somehow God gave him the grace to say nothing until his visitor spoke.) The man continued to remain silent; he simply sat there, taut, until the hour was up. At the end of the time the man looked at his watch, stood up, shook hands and said, "Thank you, Dr. Doe. It never occurred to me that another human being could

[4] Theodore O. Wedel, *The Gospel in a Strange, New World* (Philadelphia: The Westminster Press, 1963), p. 72.

endure my presence for an hour." With that he left, although this was the beginning and not the end of the counseling relationship.

Responding, or communicating, for the pastor is no major problem; he is often preacher as well as pastor. But being emotionally as well as physically "present" with a counselee—sharing the feelings that build the bridge called "rapport"—this is difficult for anyone. Listening, really *listening* to words, silences, body language as Dr. Doe did—listening with what Theodore Reik calls "the third ear"—is an art as well as a strenuous activity. It is, nevertheless, an art which pastors young and old can develop. It can be developed if one is willing to risk hearing the echo of one's own pain while listening to the pain of another. As Dr. Doe said, this may require the grace of God.

Responding to Feelings

It should be kept in mind, however, that the pastor does not listen just for the sake of listening; nor has the Christian counselor finished the job when both rapport and communication have been established. There is still another general principle of pastoral counseling, particularly important in work crises, and that is helping to bring about some *change* in the counselee. Under the heading of "Action—Essential Ingredient in Counseling," Clinebell, in *Basic Types of Pastoral Counseling,* has this to say about "change":

> Counseling in general aims at some degree of constructive change in the relationships, behavior, and functioning of persons. In addition to helping them deal with burdensome feelings, it helps them *do* something constructive about their problems and their disturbing behavior *per se.* This includes such functions as exploring alternative plans of action and helping to motivate the person to implement the most feasible plan. The latter may involve dealing with the person's inner blocks to action and even putting some judicious pressure on him to move off dead center.[5]

THE MISUSE OF METHODOLOGY

> I always say the chief end of man is to form general propositions— adding that no general proposition is worth a damn.[6]

Methodology is undoubtedly necessary in every branch of knowledge, including both the law and pastoral counseling. I, however, have been jumpy about methodology ever since I spent

---

[5] Clinebell, *op. cit.,* p. 70.
[6] Oliver Wendell Holmes, Jr., *Holmes–Pollock Letters,* ed. Mark DeWolfe Howe (Cambridge, Mass.: Harvard University Press, 1941), vol. 1, p. 13.

three years as a student at the Harvard Law School. It was probably the first graduate school to teach almost exclusively through the use of cases, here judicial opinions, rather than texts and treatises. The school then was profoundly influenced by Justice Oliver Wendell Holmes, Jr., an alumnus, former practicing lawyer and professor, legal scholar, onetime Justice and Chief Justice of the Massachusetts Supreme Court, and, finally, Justice of the Supreme Court of the United States from 1902 until his retirement in 1932 at the age of ninety.

The quotation at the beginning of this section is taken from his voluminous correspondence over more than a generation with the eminent English jurist, Sir Frederick Pollock. His remark would have shocked his Calvinist forebears, and it is easy to be picky about it today on other grounds. He was stating a general proposition, for instance, when he said that "no general proposition is worth a damn."

When Holmes discounted "general propositions," he was discounting methodology in general. Over the years as a student and practitioner of the law, he had been offended by the long misuse of legal methodology. He stated his objections more equably in a series of twelve lectures delivered in the winter of 1880–1881 to a distinguished professional group in Boston. The lectures were then published under the title of *The Common Law*. Early in the book Holmes said:

> ... The life of the law has not been logic: it has been experience. The felt necessities of the time, the prevalent moral and political theories, intuitions of public policy, avowed or unconscious, even the prejudices which judges share with their fellow-men, have had a good deal more to do than the syllogism in determining the rules by which men should be governed. The law ... cannot be dealt with as if it contained only the axioms and corollaries of a book of mathematics.[7]

One of Holmes's biographers, Catherine Drinker Bowen, in *Yankee from Olympus*, has this to say about the above quotation:

> So wrote Wendell Holmes, and *what he wrote was new*. He was deprecating formalism; he was saying that judicial decision does not derive wholly from precedent. He was saying that a good judge unconsciously predicts a law according to the result it will have upon the community at large.[8] (emphasis added)

[7] Oliver Wendell Holmes, Jr., *The Common Law* (Boston: Little, Brown and Company, 1881, 1909, 1923), p. 1.

[8] Catherine Drinker Bowen, *Yankee from Olympus* (Boston: Little, Brown & Co., 1944), p. 275.

A close reading of the two quotations above is warranted. Holmes's biographer wrote that "judicial decision does not derive *wholly* from precedent." He himself said that the law "cannot be dealt with as if it contained *only* the axioms and corollaries of a book of mathematics." This is a far cry from saying one need not know the general principles, the methodology, of the law—or pastoral counseling. Holmes could be cavalier about general principles only because he and those to whom he was lecturing knew them well. He used "the pedagogue's license to exaggerate" to impress upon his listeners and later his readers the necessity of being controlled by "the felt necessities" rather than general principles where a choice had to be made. And the same could be said regarding the primacy, "the felt necessities" of pastoral counseling.

Listening, for example, helps the counselor determine what the needs of the counselee are; listening also gives the counselee an opportunity to ventilate, in a kind of cathartic way, the feelings which prevent focusing on the problem at hand. Listening also indicates the counselor's care and concern for the counselee which is needed to establish their relationship. The pastor, therefore, who knows the needs of the counselee and who already has a good relationship with the counselee, will sometimes interrupt and be quite directive. An example of this is found in the second case study of chapter 2 of this book. In that instance, Mrs. Markham's first response to Karen was: "First of all, shut up and calm down and *listen to me.*" Mrs. Markham already had a good relationship with Karen, and she quickly realized where Karen was; she knew that Karen's first need was to be pulled out of a spin that could lead to hysteria rather than to consideration of the problem at hand.

The misuse of methodology is not cured by ignorance of methodology. It is cured when it is subordinated to the needs of the counselee if the occasion demands it. An effective counselor usually knows the methodology of counseling; the same counselor also realizes that it is valuable only insofar as it meets the needs of the particular counselee at a particular time. The good pastor, like the good surgeon, knows the old saying: "The operation was a success, but the patient died!"

Analogies between legal and pastoral methodology cannot be precise. A pastor, for example, can only suggest that a counselee consider the possibility of a changed approach to a problem. On the other hand, a judge can change a situation on his or her own initiative and enforce it, externally at least. In spite of all the differences, however, a counselor's ears might well prick up on hearing Holmes's biographer say, "Law only ends with a theory; it begins with a concrete case."[9]

Surely a pastor having what Wedel calls "an incarnational theology" would hear the ring, not of the whole truth, but of at least a partial truth in the statement. But theology is the subject of the next section.

THE EFFECT OF THEOLOGY ON THE METHODOLOGY OF COUNSELING IN WORK CRISES

> All human beings always have lived, do now and always will live, by some kind of story, some kind of plot, some kind of drama in which they know themselves to be actors on a stage (Theodore O. Wedel).[10]

The book just quoted consists of a series of five informal lectures Wedel had given to lay people ten years earlier. His purpose was to present the Bible as a five-act drama with a plot people can place themselves in and live by. Following the sentence just quoted, he says in the Introduction:

> . . . . Whatever else man is, he is an acting being: he is a person who makes decisions; he has to exercise freedom. Even when freedom can philosophically be proved to be an illusion, he still acts as though he is free. And, granted freedom, granted that man has to act, that he has to make decisions, he has to make those decisions by some kind of design.
> If man has no other design, he will create one for himself. As a matter of fact, the drama that a good many people live by is simply a drama of their own making in which they are not only the chief actors but also the stage managers and the writers of the plot. Egocentricity is self-worship: "I am the center of the universe, and my career is the story by which I live." (That pattern will emerge a little more clearly when we come to the problem of the Fall.) But there have been other great plots and great stories by which men have lived. Let me sketch a few of them for you.[11]

Wedel then sketches briefly the "plots" of Buddhism, of the polytheistic religion of the ancient Greeks, of modern Communism, and of the French existentialism of Sartre and others who proclaim that life is "absurd." In the body of the book he goes through the Christian plot; he takes up serially the five acts he finds in the biblical drama, beginning with creation, and ending with the final

[9] *Ibid.*, p. 287.
[10] Theodore O. Wedel, *The Drama of the Bible* (Cincinnati: Forward Movement Publications, 1965), p. 17.
[11] *Ibid.*

consummation because, he says, "It is the end which gives every drama its meaning." [12] To Wedel the Bible is "a love story"—the story of the relationship, the covenant, between God and the human beings God created in his own image—a love story that begins with a divorce, the Fall. In the end God "woos back" the offending people whom he created and whom he loves eternally.

One may consider simplistic Wedel's approach to the Bible and Christian theology as restated here. It is difficult, however, to challenge his basic assertion that all people live by some kind of design. This assertion has substantial implications for both the purpose and the methodology of all Christian counseling, including pastoral counseling in work crises. When Christian theology says that people can live "more abundantly" by the Christian story, it is saying more than that; Christian theology is also saying, certainly by implication, that the counselor's task should be designed to help the counselee live into—find an appropriate place in—the Christian story.

To describe the pastor's task in different words, it is to help the counselee be open to receive an answer to the familiar prayer, written by Reinhold Niebuhr and adopted by Alcoholics Anonymous: "God, give me the serenity to endure those things which cannot be changed, the courage to change those things which ought to be changed, and the wisdom to know one from the other." Living into the Christian story may bring one counselee serenity to endure the unchangeable or courage to make necessary changes or wisdom for discernment. The pastor's task in the process has often been compared to that of a midwife in childbirth.

Take, for instance, the case of a counselee whose design for life was the first described by Wedel: a person who has "created a design for himself"—a design where "I am the center of the universe, and my career is the story by which I live." For the pastor to *understand* this design and accept the counselee in spite of it is one thing; but to *confirm* this position is quite another. The latter was the methodology of the prophets of Baal, of whom Jeremiah wrote: "They say continually to those who despise the word of the Lord, 'It shall be well with you'; and to every one who stubbornly follows his own heart, they say, 'No evil shall come upon you'" (Jeremiah 23:17).

The pastor can disclaim an ability to be of any assistance in working out a design which places the counselee in the center of the

[12] *Ibid.*, p. 106.

universe—one in which the counselee's career is the story by which he or she wants to live. At the same time the counselee can be assured of the pastor's desire to help should the counselee ever wish to live into the Christian story. At some future time the counselee might well discern that the responsibilities that go with being God are both awesome and impossible. Since the pastor had left the door open, the counselee might then, like the prodigal son, come back simply as a child of God and a loving member of his family.

I have wondered whether, given the opportunity, I would have been able to "understand" but "not confirm" my friend, Mark, during a pilgrimage Mark made in midlife. With more insight at the time, I might have been able to counsel him fifteen years ago, shortly after an incident that may have precipitated my friend's journey. I was staying for an evening with Mark and his wife in an area where he was working as the regional executive for a large corporation. He had gone to work for the company and married shortly after his graduation from college. At the time of the visit Mark was almost fifty, and one of his duties was interviewing college seniors in the area who were interested in the possibility of going to work for the same company. His account of a recent interview struck me as simply an amusing story of a callow youth. Mark told how he had completed his questioning of one senior and asked if there were any questions he would like to ask. The young man replied: "There is only one. Why aren't you president of this corporation? You obviously have more of everything than I do—background, intelligence, presence, looks, voice—and I don't want to go to work for a company where I don't at least have a *chance* of becoming president." Mark said that he took the question quite seriously and, after thinking a moment, replied, "I don't know; I have never been asked that question before. It may be because I have been more of a family man than a company man. I have turned down a good many assignments and some promotions because I did not want to uproot my family."

It was not long after the incident that Mark resigned from the company. His children by then were all on their own or in college, and he was financially independent because of the profit-sharing stock bonuses he had received from the corporation over the years. His former widespread interests began to narrow into a long-suppressed concern for himself, and his chief activity became work on a neglected hobby. Not too long afterwards, he got a divorce from his wife.

His loving, outgoing nature reasserted itself, however, and he

married another woman and settled in a different city where he still
pursues his hobby, but is once again a caring, concerned member of
his church and community.

At the other end of the theological spectrum might be a
counselee who has become convinced that "life is absurd," who is
reacting to a long series of unfortunate work crises and believes that
he or she must be some kind of a cosmic joke or accident. To the mind
of the pastor in this situation might come the words another great
prophet spoke to a people who felt like that counselee:

> Remember these things, O Jacob,
>> and Israel, for you are my servant;
> I formed you, you are my servant;
>> O Israel, you will not be forgotten
>> by me.
> I have swept away your transgressions
>> like a cloud,
>> and your sins like mist;
> return to me, for I have redeemed you.
>> Isaiah 44:21-22

In such a situation, however, it may not be words which the
counselee's self-esteem needs; it may be that the love and acceptance
of the pastor can come across better through listening and just being
"present" with the counselee. In the lovely Christmas carol "O Little
Town of Bethlehem," Phillips Brooks wrote:

> How silently, how silently,
> The wondrous gift is given!

If the great gift of God's love was given silently on the first Christmas,
perhaps it may be shared silently today. The *words* of the Christian
story can come later, should the pastor be asked questions. Dr. Doe's
visitor, in Wedel's illustration several pages back, must have asked
later about the source of the love and acceptance he received. When
such questions are asked, the pastor can then tell the Christian story
and add that the counselee might consider changing and being "a
good steward" of the talent he or she has also been given.

Somewhere in the spectrum of counselees is the person in an
insoluble work crisis, caused by age or infirmity or some other factor
that cannot be changed. The following case study may be more
suggestive of an appropriate methodology in that situation than
anything which the author could write. The case is verbatim, written
several years ago by a pastor unknown to the author, for an unknown

group of clergy in the Washington area who met regularly to reflect on pastoral procedures. While the crisis here was that of an impending, painful death, the same methodology might be used by a pastor trying to help a counselee find "the serenity to endure" an insoluble work crisis. There are some insoluble work crises that promise a painful kind of living death if they are unrelieved by the transforming power of Christian love and faith.

Sally W. is a woman of 40 who was once attractive, but is now almost a mere skeleton covered by flesh, weighing about 60 pounds, and wasting away from cancer. However, she is still mentally alert and is able to discuss not only her own predicament, but still takes a lively interest in the world around her.

I have known Sally for about 15 months, visiting her several times each week either at her home or in the hospital. During this period she has retired from her job in the government and is now unable to leave her bed. Sally lives with her parents who care for her during her illness, both suffering from this close contact with their daughter's misery. Sally never married and has worked overseas in Alaska and Argentina, toured Europe, has been interested in hobbies ranging from photography to raising flowers and farm animals.

We have talked over the meaning of life and death in general and specifically in terms of her own illness. But I never know what to expect from her for one time she is resigned to her fate and on my next visit she will be making plans for the future. She is able to retain but little of her food and struggles to eat in order to maintain her strength.

The visit I will report happened last week. I called at her home, a neat ranch-type home located on a ridge with a beautiful view of the countryside. When I called through the open kitchen door with my customary greeting, I was met by Sally's mother who told me, "She is in a bad way. I am so glad you have come."

She described Sally's condition and told me she was having violent headaches and nausea. She then took me to her room and Sally was struggling to keep from vomiting.

I raised her head while her mother held the pan and after she threw up her mother left the room.

She said, "Andy, I am sorry you have to see me like this."

I replied: "It doesn't matter."

"Of course it matters. Don't you think I am a woman? I hate this. I hate God for allowing me to go on like this," she replied.

I then held her hand while she cried softly for about five minutes.

When she stopped crying I dried her eyes and released her hand and said, "This is quite a change from when I saw you yesterday."

"You mean about God?"

"No, I mean your vomiting and headache. You were feeling pretty good when I left you yesterday."

She replied that it had started about an hour after I left.

Then, looking directly at me she said, "I've suffered enough. I'm not afraid to die, in fact I would welcome it," and she kept repeating over and over, "I want to die. Why won't your God let me die?"

All of my previous efforts to reconcile the idea of sin and sickness with a just and good God came flooding into my head.

And echoing in my brain were her words—why won't *your* God let me die?

Sure, He is my God, but He is also hers, I thought. Why hold me responsible for Him?

These musings were interrupted when she said, "Andy, God is no damn good."

How could I look at such agony, hurt and misery and still say, "Yes, God is good."

I couldn't, so I reached out and held her hand again.

As I sat there outwardly calm, but suffering with her inwardly, she said, "Andy, I don't mean it, but I hurt so. You don't know how I hurt. Nobody does."

"Will you pray with me?" she asked.

I quietly said the Lord's Prayer and thought, she doesn't want her daily bread, she wants death.

When I finished, I suggested that she lie quietly and not talk, for this would make her headache worse.

She nodded and I again removed my hand from hers and, as she attempted to get more comfortable by changing position, I shifted to my favorite rocker. I sat there for 15 minutes rocking quietly and as Sally seemed to rest I felt comfortable for the first time during the visit.

She appeared to fall asleep; and as I started to leave she spoke, asking if I was mad with her.

"How could I ever be mad with you?" I replied.

"I mean about God."

"Sally, I'm pretty mad at Him myself right now. I'll see you tomorrow, and I won't try to say anything stupid like 'rest well.' I don't see how I can say my usual 'God bless you and keep you.'"

She answered, "Say it anyway, will you?"

"God bless you and keep you this night and for evermore, Sally."

I walked to the kitchen and, as her mother asked me a question, she started to cry. I couldn't talk. I was too busy crying myself, and I didn't mind the crying, but I was afraid I would start sobbing, so we shook hands and I left without a word.

It is easy to pick out in the foregoing incident the things which the pastor might have done or left undone. The fact is, however, that Andy shared the love of God with Sally; he got across to her that she was not alone and that he knew her doubts and fears.

Andy also articulated and confirmed her faith that "God would bless her and keep her this night and for evermore." The promise that "God shall wipe away all tears from their eyes" (Revelation 7:17) can begin to come true here and now in insoluble work crises, as it did with Sally. This is not the kind of counseling professional career guidance counselors are privy to, and it is seldom referred to in books on the subject. But insoluble work crises are familiar to the pastor.

There is no questioning Sally's pain and distress as she faces physical death from cancer. It may seem to be stretching a point even to compare an insoluble work crisis to hers or to suggest that the same kind of Christian love and faith is needed if a person is to endure a *work* crisis with serenity. But listen to the American Medical Association's Committee on Aging speak on compulsory retirement:

.... Forces outside of medicine inflict a disease-or disability-producing condition upon working men and women that is no less devastating than cancer, tuberculosis, or heart disease. This condition—enforced idleness—robs those affected of the will to live full, well-rounded lives, deprives them of opportunities for compelling physical and mental activity, and encourages atrophy and decay. It robs the worker of his initiative and independence. It narrows physical and mental horizons so much that the patient's final interests and compulsions are in grumbling about his complaints.[13]

[13] *Retirement—A Medical Philosophy and Approach* (Chicago: American Medical Association, 1972), pp. 1-2.

6

Utilizing Opportunities
for Pastoral Counseling
in Work Crises

THE PASTOR'S APPROACH TO COUNSELING IN WORK CRISES

Whatever is worth doing at all, is
worth doing poorly.
                    G. K. Chesterton

In his wry manner Chesterton was here protesting Lord
Chesterfield's earlier counsel: "Whatever is worth doing at all, is
worth doing well." [1] It is Chesterfield's counsel that society generally
offers today; and it can paralyze people, including pastors—people
who see a need, who want to do something about it, but who might
not do it "well," not in the beginning anyhow. The result is that
pastors, like other well-intentioned people, may never begin doing all
they could to meet the needs, in this case, of people in work crises.

Chesterton could have quoted Scripture (which he knew well) to
make the same point. For Paul was thanking the Christians at
Philippi for their "active partnership in the gospel" when he wrote:
"He who began a good work in you will bring it to completion at the

[1] Philip Dormer Stanhope, Earl of Chesterfield, *Letters* (March 10, 1746), as quoted
in John Bartlett, *Familiar Quotations*, ed. Emily Morison Beck (Boston: Little, Brown
and Company, 1968), p. 415.

day of Jesus Christ" (Philippians 1:6). Pastors can take heart from Paul's conviction that our Lord is not only "the pioneer and perfecter of our faith" (Hebrews 12:2) but also of the work begun in that faith.

Work crisis counseling will be presented in this chapter through situations rather than through theories. Looking at situations may encourage pastors to begin approaching work crises with the counseling skills they have already developed in other crises, where the only difference was the nature of the particular crisis.

Some pastors might prefer to approach counseling in work crises through further study of the various *types* of counseling. For them there are other books which offer that approach far better than I can, one of them being the frequently cited work of Howard J. Clinebell, Jr., *Basic Types of Pastoral Counseling*. In this book Clinebell devotes an entire chapter to each of twelve different types of counseling. Another alternative approach to counseling in work crises is further study of the various *functions* of ministry. A useful book on that subject is *Pastoral Care in Historical Perspective*[2] by William Clebsch and Charles Jaekle. The authors there identify four classic pastoral functions: healing, sustaining, guiding, and reconciling. The book points out that all four functions are operative and developing today.

The situations which will be considered here are grouped in five categories that emphasize, in turn: *Who* is counseling and being counseled? *What* is the nature of the work crisis involved? *When* does the counseling take place? *Where* is the counseling available? and *Why* is the counseling done? There was an old axiom in the newspaper business which said that the lead paragraph in every news story should answer the questions "Who?" "What?" "When?" and "Where?" The assumption was that, having been given quick answers to these questions, the reader would be led into reading the body of the article where, if it were good journalism, there would also be an answer to the question "Why?" The same kind of quick coverage of counseling situations in various kinds of work crises is offered here, with the intent that ordained and lay pastors may be led into the *practice* of such counseling as well as its *theory*.

Dean Krister Stendahl of the Harvard Divinity School could have been addressing seminaries and congregations alike in his "Report to the President of the University, 1975-76." He was

---

[2] William Clebsch and Charles Jaekle, *Pastoral Care in Historical Perspective*, reprint of 1946 edition (New York: Jason Aronson, Inc., 1975).

deploring the growing distance between the "major independent and university-centered divinity schools" and the churches. He wrote:

> If it has not yet happened in the churches, then it has not happened yet. Until the insights that become ours through study and reflection, through finds and findings, have become incarnate in the life and faith and worship and spirituality of the communities of faith, we just have not done our job.[3]

One could be more specific and add that until pastoral counseling in work crises moves out of the books and into the life and work of pastors and congregations, "it has not happened yet."

WHO IS COUNSELING AND BEING COUNSELED?

> [Jesus] replied, "Who are my mother and my brothers?" And looking around on those who sat about him, he said, "Here are my mother and my brothers! Whoever does the will of God is my brother, and sister, and mother" (Mark 3:33-35).

There is a good bit of this kind of pragmatism in the Synoptic Gospels of Matthew, Mark, and Luke, as there is in the prophetic tradition of the Old Testament. So it may be in order to say here that all those who wrestle in the Christian spirit with work crises, whether attempting to help or receive help, are the counselors and counselees for whom this book is written. The counselors may be ordained or unordained pastors; the counselees may be within or without the institutional church. It is the spirit which governs the action that makes the counseling "pastoral."

Ordained pastors can begin work crisis counseling generally *without* any specific counselee. Preaching and teaching are obvious ways to help people identify and acknowledge the existence of their work crises. Congregations can also be assured that it is not demeaning to be in such a crisis; and they can be told as a group where helpful people and materials are available, including the pastor's study.

There is also available to interested pastors the ministry of the printed word. The parish bulletin, mailed to an entire congregation, is an old standby for communicating with all church members regardless of their attendance at services. Helpful bulletins go even further; they have a way of getting themselves mailed to relatives and friends of members. Then there is the "tract rack," located in the vestibules of many church buildings. There are excellent pamphlets

[3] Dean Krister Stendahl, "Report to the President of the University, 1975-76," p. 4.

and booklets available for display, such as Richard N. Bolles's little pamphlet, *Take Heart—A Word to the Unemployed*.[4]

Of course, pastoral counseling in work crises, like other kinds of counseling, normally takes place in personal consultations. Here pastors could do most of their counseling in work crises in the same way that they do in other crisis situations. In work crises, however, the ordained pastor need not be the only member of the counseling team. Here the lay pastors have an unusually important role to play because of their own experience and their acquaintances in the lines of work that interest the counselee. They can be the counselor of first instance, like Mrs. Markham in the second case study in chapter 2, with the ordained pastor standing by as a resource person; or the lay pastors can be on a roster of counselors to whom the ordained pastor feels free to make referrals. One pastor writes:

> Currently an elder of our congregation is establishing an unemployment counseling service for the purpose not only of helping people to find work but also to support them and offer some sense of hope during the traumatic experience of being out-of-work.[5]

Referral counseling may be one of the chief functions of the pastor when people come for help in work crises. Experienced pastors have always known that referral of a counselee need not mean the withdrawal of the pastor from the situation. Judicious referral by the pastor can easily be treated as bringing a specialist "on the team" of which the pastor remains a working member, or at least a standby member. The same principle applies when the pastor refers a counselee to a professional agency or institution for career guidance—or when the pastor recommends materials for the counselee who seeks "self-help" in the resolution of a work crisis.

There are great possibilities for mutual counseling within a group of people who are considering their present work crises or such impending crises as retirement. Most of the materials prepared for self-help in these situations are used more effectively by groups of at least two or three; and some of the courses designed by Aid for Independent Maturity, the arm of the American Association of Retired Persons alluded to earlier, are specifically intended for groups. Their seminar materials, for example, are geared to a

---

[4] Richard N. Bolles, *Take Heart—A Word to the Unemployed* (Cincinnati: Forward Movement Publications, 1972, and 1975).

[5] Edward W. Castner, "A Theology of Ministry," *The Drew Gateway* (Madison, N.J.: Drew University, 1976-77), vol. 47, no.1, p. 69.

minimum of twenty people meeting for at least eight sessions to plan their forthcoming retirement.

The important fact is that the pastor is functioning as a counselor whether the method used is the "spray-gun" technique (with sermons, classroom teaching, or the printed word), the holding of individual consultations, the making of referrals to informed lay pastors or professional guidance counselors, or the helping of individuals or groups to make use of prepared materials.

The counselees, in turn, are any who make use of the direct or indirect assistance made available by the ordained or lay pastorate.

WHAT IS THE NATURE OF THE WORK CRISIS?

So I saw that there is nothing better than that a man should enjoy his work, for that is his lot . . . (Ecclesiastes 3:22).

An attempt was made in chapter 2 to define "work crises" generally. Although it was noted that all work crises would be considered together in this book, the distinction was made between the work crisis of late adolescence, a "developmental" crisis, and all the other work crises, which are usually "accidental."

The distinction may be helpful in considering the nature of work crises, because the crisis of late adolescence or young adulthood is the only one which a pastor can anticipate *all* people having to go through. It can become acute, at least in middle and upper income groups, when young people face the end of their formal education and their entry into mature work relationships. Young people in lower income groups often face this crisis at a different time if economic necessity forces them to leave school and begin working at a much earlier age.

Time will show whether the impact of this crisis in the teens and twenties can be substantially lessened by the career guidance now being offered at colleges and universities. Such assistance is gradually being made available to young people further and further down the age-scale. Some junior high schools now provide guidance counselors to help children who want to discuss, among other things, their future work life before selecting courses in high school. The state of Virginia's Department of Education, through its Division of Vocational Education, even developed in 1977 a course intended to help sixth grade children "look at individual personality characteristics as they relate to work selection." Under the heading "Course Design" the prospectus for the course states:

A World of Choice: Careers and You is designed to be taught for either one semester or a full year, with four major emphases:

1. An initial emphasis on *self* understanding as it pertains to work.
2. Understanding and simulating *work modes,* or the styles in which people work.
3. Identification and simulation of the work models found in all categories of work, using the 15 USOE *occupational clusters.*
4. Synthesis of all previous experiences in light of *planning* for future exploratory courses, as well as out-of-school experiences.[6]

While it is heartening to see educators taking the work crises of young people seriously, there are great numbers of late adolescents and young adults who remain in unresolved work crises today. Many of them have had warm relationships with a pastor as they were growing up. No one can say what percentage of them would discuss their current problems with the pastor whom they knew to be concerned about them and about work crises, but experience has shown that the number could be considerable.

The following case may be fairly typical.

Sam is a young man of twenty-four who has known the pastor well for a number of years. He graduated from college over a year ago, having majored in philosophy with a minor in religious studies. Shortly after graduation he talked to the pastor about the possibility of doing graduate work in religious studies. He thought that this would give him a chance to test his interest in the subject; graduate work could also be a step toward teaching religious studies if his undergraduate interest deepened.

Sam's parents had both been to graduate school, and his father was a lawyer, following the family tradition of either law or teaching. His parents were willing and financially able to send Sam to graduate school, but they were dubious about his interest in a subject as vague as "religion," since he did not want to go into the ordained ministry. Sam also questioned his own commitment to the subject; he realized that he might be using graduate school, at considerable cost to his parents, to postpone any real decision as to a career. He had little interest in the law and did not seem unhappy that he had been turned down at law school after doing poorly on his legal aptitude test.

The pastor discussed career planning generally with him and found that Sam was not interested in going to a career guidance

[6]From "A World of Choice: Careers and You," published by the Department of Education of the State of Virginia, Division of Vocational Education, in 1977.

center for professional help. He did accept a book and Richard N. Bolles's *The Quick Job-Hunting Map,*[7] a booklet with exercises designed to help one identify interests, skills, and aptitudes. He was also willing to confer with a mutual friend, a professor of religious studies at the college level, about possible graduate schools. At Sam's request the pastor also wrote a letter recommending him for such graduate study, to be placed in his file at his college's personnel office.

A month or so later the pastor received a letter from Sam, saying how much he appreciated the pastor's help but that he had come to the conclusion that he was not yet ready to make any long-term decisions about a career. Instead, he had taken a job in a bank in a nearby community where he had a good many friends and acquaintances. The job would pay enough for him to live without family support.

About a year later Sam came to see the pastor again. Their conversation went like this:

Pastor: Sam, I hear you've moved across the country and are now living in San Francisco.

Sam: Yeah—I'm just home to be in a cousin's wedding. I drew on my savings account and made the trip as a kind of wedding present to him.

Pastor: What happened at the bank?

Sam: There were too many little details for me—and, besides, I had no real interest in it. I got a ride to San Francisco, where I had a couple of friends. You will never guess what I am doing there. I am an apprentice to an Italian who repairs antiques and other fine furniture.

Pastor: Tell me some more.

Sam: Well, he also makes copies of antique tables and things. I am not very good, but there is a lot I *can* do.

Pastor: Sam, have you ever done much woodworking before?

Sam: Oh, I used to hang around carpenters—and a woodworking shop—but I was probably more of a nuisance than a help.

Pastor: Do you ever think about making a career out of this kind of thing?

Sam: I don't think I would want to spend my life at this kind of

[7] Richard N. Bolles, *The Quick Job-Hunting Map* (Berkeley, Calif.: Ten Speed Press, 1976).

work. And I am just not ready to make any lifetime commitment, anyhow.

Pastor: Does that include commitments to girls, too?

Sam: Yeah. I was beginning to see a lot of one girl in San Francisco, but we broke up.

Pastor: Sam, I don't mean to offend you, but let me check something out with you: You sound to me like you are fairly passive about your life—willing just to let things happen.

Sam: I guess I am right now. I still may end up going to law school.

Pastor: I know another fellow who got interested in very much the same kind of work you are doing. He is now finishing up graduate work in fine arts and restorations, looking forward to going into museum work.

Sam: Well, I had better be getting back to the house. It has been good talking to you again . . .

Pastor: Sam, if you ever feel that you have some kind of a block against making decisions that you would like to get rid of, let me know. I have a good psychiatrist friend who will see people once or twice, just for an evaluation—to see whether some kind of psychiatric help might be useful. He could even recommend someone in San Francisco you could get an evaluation from without any long-term commitment.

Sam: That's good to know. I have some friends who have really been helped by therapy. Well . . . my family doesn't know where I am, and I know they are expecting me for lunch. But I'll keep in touch with you.

Other work crises, being "accidental," tend to have more in common with one another than they do with such "developmental" crises as the above, despite their great diversity. Other work crises, for instance, do not usually arise from an underdeveloped emotional ability to enter into a mature work relationship; they are more often the result of a person not having an obvious opportunity to make a commitment to such a relationship. This could easily be true of the unemployed or the retired person. Where the work crisis is job dissatisfaction, an opportunity to enter a more enjoyable work relationship might be taken away by financial commitments that rule out a lower salary or a financial risk. In the same way, a housewife's opportunity to reenter the job market might be taken away by overriding family pressures.

One of the most common factors in work crises, whether precipitated by work dissatisfaction or by termination of a previous job, is the failure to recognize one's ability to meet job opportunities which either exist or could be created. Time and again this failure is the result of people's belief that they are qualified only for work that carries their old job description. Bernard Haldane has illustrated this factor with an account of a consultation with a young man just returned from Peace Corps service in South America.[8] It was the only job the returnee had held since leaving school. He told Haldane that he wanted to go back to the Bronx in New York to work; his Peace Corps job had been the artificial insemination of cattle, but, he added wistfully, "there is not much market for that in the Bronx." Haldane pressed his counselee to describe all the duties the South American job entailed. The young man explained how he had to organize those who raised low-grade cattle in one area and those who raised breeding stock in another area and how he worked out the logistics that permitted them to do business with each other. After listening carefully, his wise counselor explained to the young man how, his job description aside, he had really been doing community organization all the time and that nowhere was community organization more needed than in the Bronx. As you may guess, this case had a happy ending.

The same failure to recognize employable skills is common in the case of women whose job description has been "housewife" ever since they left school and were married. When their children have reached school age, and these women want a job outside the house, they can be frustrated by the conviction that they have had no work experience other than raising children and looking after a house. A concerned pastor can, like Bernard Haldane, go over with them the various activities these duties entail. Skills may surface that vary from pastry cooking to preparation of income tax returns, many of them marketable without even further training!

WHEN DOES THE COUNSELING TAKE PLACE?

For everything there is a season, and a time for every matter under heaven: . . . a time to break down, and a time to build up (Ecclesiastes 3:1-3b).

---

[8] Haldane also refers briefly to the incident in his book *Career Satisfaction and Success: A Guide to Job Freedom*, ed. William Olcheski (New York: AMACOM, a division of American Management Associations, 1974), pp. 129-130.

Pastoral counseling in work crises can take place over an extended period of time, as in Sam's case, or a very short one. In the two cases that follow, the very brief counseling took place while the counselees were in quite different work situations: in the first, the counselee was thinking of leaving an unsatisfactory work relationship; in the second, the counselee was getting psychiatric help to remove the emotional blocks that kept her from enjoying her work in an otherwise satisfactory work relationship.

I unwittingly precipitated the first counseling episode. I was visiting in another city and having dinner with six young men and women. All of them were in their late twenties and early thirties, and all were working. When the conversation turned to the book that I was then writing, I asked the group, "How many of you are in work crises now?" Five of the six said that they were in such a crisis for one reason or another. One of the young women, whom I had not known before, asked me to have lunch with her the next day. She brought up the subject of her crisis at the luncheon table.

Judy: Do you think I am crazy to be thinking about leaving my job and going after another graduate degree, this time in business administration?

Pastor: I don't really know anything about your present job except that it is with a big construction company. Could you tell me some more about it?

Judy: Well, I went to work for them when I left the university. I had a double master's degree in economics, that is, in two different branches of the subject. I was also a Teaching Fellow and got a lot of satisfaction out of teaching. Anyhow, the company has taken good care of me and pushed me right along. I am now in charge of preparing the bids which we make for new work.

Pastor: It sounds to me like you have a very significant job and that you are really appreciated.

Judy: I am, and that is one of the things that makes the decision hard—in fact, I have just been given another raise.

Pastor: What are some of the bad things about it?

Judy: The main thing is the incompetence of the people in the various departments who supply the figures I compile for the bids. The really good people are out of the office on various jobs. Only two bids out of the last fifty I have prepared have been successful. There is just no satisfaction for me in that kind of sloppy work.

Pastor: I think I can understand that, but could you effect any changes in the procedures now being used?

Judy: I couldn't bring about any change because the difficulty is not the system we use but the people.

Pastor: Well, tell me about the other side. What makes going to business school attractive—more so, say, than another job?

Judy: I feel like I am too narrow as a person. My education, both on the undergraduate and the graduate school levels, has been limited to a very narrow field. In spite of the fact that I was a Phi Beta Kappa and all of that, I never had a liberal education. There are people I respect who sometimes tell me that.

Pastor: Are you saying you would take this radical step because of what a few people think?

Judy: Oh, what some people say is not the real reason; it just happens to be true. And I could never teach—not even economics—without the kind of broader-based education I would get at business school. I got a lot of satisfaction out of teaching.

Pastor: What about the money for all this?

Judy: I have saved some money; I am not married and I am a hard worker. For instance, I made money over and above the cost of graduate school, running a little business of my own while I was there. Of course there is still a question about my being admitted to business school; I have not yet heard from my Business School Aptitude Tests.

Pastor: Are you honestly worried about passing them?

Judy: Well, you never know until you hear from the exams; but I guess I am mainly worried about using the company I work for. I have never told them that I took my B.S.A.T.'s or that I was considering leaving. In the meantime I recently accepted another raise.

Pastor: Would you leave them time to find a replacement for you?

Judy: Oh, sure.

Pastor: I am not just trying to make you feel good about it, but have you anything definite to talk to them about—or any real decision to make—until you hear from your aptitude tests?

Judy: Maybe I don't—they have just been so good about everything that I have been worrying.

Pastor: Well, it seems to me that you have a responsibility to hear them out—really to listen to them—as soon as you do know what your options are. And maybe you should level with them—honestly. Even if you leave, you might be able to repay them with a report on what is happening in your office.

Judy: That helps.

Judy did pass her aptitude tests and is going to business school, which reminds me that perhaps the Preacher of Ecclesiastes was correct in saying "there is a time to break down."

The "time to build" came to mind when a former student recounted to me the following conversation he had had with another able young woman. They had been friends at college. She had been rising rapidly in a publishing firm while he had been preparing for ordination at seminary. In this case, the young woman, who was unmarried, enjoyed her work but was frightened by her success. The young pastor reported this part of the conversation they had had when they met recently for the first time in a number of years:

Woman: I'm scared, I tell you.

Pastor: What are you afraid of?

Woman: They have been promoting me so fast.

Pastor: What is so scary about that?

Woman: Suppose I fall on my face? The publishing business *is* a male-oriented business, you know. My company is, anyhow, and I know that some of the men resent my last promotion.

Pastor: Look—I know you from way back in college; and you would not be you if you were *not* working hard and doing a good job.

Woman: You are right that I just can't goof off—and I enjoy the work—but I also need to sleep at night and not worry about having risen too fast.

Pastor: Are you doing anything about that?

Woman: Yes, I have started seeing a psychiatrist regularly.

Pastor: Great! Stay with the psychiatrist. Too many of us are carrying around fears and worries that a good therapist can help us get rid of. But I would say that you should stay with any outfit that is smart enough to recognize your ability.

Here were two situations where the question was not finding a job or doing it well; the problem was the failure of these two women, both highly competent, to enjoy the work they were doing. Judy resolved her crisis by breaking off the work relationship to broaden her own education; this would give her the options, possibly, of teaching or going into another business. The other woman seemed to be on the way to enjoying the same work through what Bolles calls "dealing with her interior furniture." Bolles breaks down professional help with one's personal growth into three categories: Instruction, Exploration, and Psychotherapy.[9] The young woman in the second case had, probably wisely, chosen psychotherapy.

WHERE IS THE COUNSELING AVAILABLE?

In the days of the old sailing vessels, a ship had been becalmed off the coast of South America for a long time. The ship's supply of fresh water was almost exhausted, and the crew was becoming desperate. When another vessel drifted near enough to receive a signal, the captain of the first ship asked if they had any fresh water to spare. The message came back, "Let down your buckets." The ship had drifted into the mouth of the Amazon River, and, although no land was in sight, they were floating on fresh water.

The late Edwin A. Penick, bishop of the Episcopal diocese of North Carolina, was fond of telling the above story to illustrate his belief that salvation is often at hand where we least expect it: right where we are. The story is used here to make the point that help for people in work crises can also be made available to them right where they are: in the average congregation and community.

Bolles, in *What Color Is Your Parachute?* titles his fourth chapter "What About Getting Help?" He stresses the importance of job hunters doing some work on their own before turning to any resources. For example, job hunting on one's own provides information as to what one knows and does not know about the process. This knowledge equips the same person to know what help is needed from others. After one knows what is needed, Bolles recommends:

1. *books, pamphlets, and other printed materials* (e.g., his own work, *What Color Is Your Parachute?*)
2. *free professional help,* such as librarians, nearby university resources, chambers of commerce, business friends, etc.

[9] Richard N. Bolles, *What Color Is Your Parachute?* (Berkeley, Calif.: Ten Speed Press, 1977), pp. 221-226.

3. *professional help for a fee,* which he considers a final resort, and then only after one has done considerable research on the professional person.[10]

And the pastor is by no means the only source of help. Invaluable help can be given by lay support groups, organized by ordained or lay pastors to meet the various needs of those who might "let down their buckets." A group of young people who had recently made their way successfully into the job market could be called, for instance, to counsel other young people who were now trying to find their way; a group of men and women who had found satisfying work after a period of unemployment could give both help and hope to others now unemployed; other groups with appropriate experience could counsel older women who had been involved in household duties but now wanted or needed outside work, or people who were in or facing a work crisis because of retirement.

The time and place of such local counseling, whether by the pastor or support groups, would vary according to the particular situations. At the Life-Work Shops which he directs for the National Career Development Project of United Ministries in Higher Education, Richard N. Bolles often uses a chart to illustrate the variety of places where work crisis counseling can take place. He goes by the amount of time the counselor has with the counselee, and he lists the following time blocks:

Passing By
Five Minutes
An Hour or So
A Day Workshop
A Weekend or So
16 Weeks or So

In all the time blocks except "Passing By," he suggests usable tools to help counselees find their own answers to WHAT their main worries are, WHERE occupational information can be gathered, and HOW one goes about getting a job. Even in "Passing By," Bolles suggests that a pamphlet like *Take Heart* (see page 60) can be handed out and a book can be recommended.

For those who are involved in the "do-it-yourself" method in work crises, then books, pamphlets, and written exercises can be made available. The same holds true for directories of guidance

[10] *Ibid.,* pp. 47-48.

counselors and centers when referral for professional help is indicated and manageable.

There are two activities, however, in which the pastor does seem to be indispensable. The first activity, already discussed in the opening chapter of this book, is that of effecting a change in the climate of a congregation where members are hesitant to mention their work crises. The second activity that normally calls for the pastor's opportunities and resources is that of helping individuals recognize and admit the existence of their work crises. It seems relatively easy to tell the pastor that one is troubled—pastors hear this in the aisles of supermarkets as well as in their studies. Yet it seems to be difficult or demeaning for numbers of people to go beyond the symptoms of their problems and identify their cause as the lack of a satisfying work relationship.

Helping people identify and admit the existence of a basic problem is a pastoral counselor's art, just as diagnosing the cause of a patient's ostensible physical difficulties is one of the physician's arts. My father was a physician who attended medical school in New Orleans around 1900. He often told the story of the summer vacation he spent as ship's surgeon on a freighter sailing from that port to Europe and back. A ship's surgeon was required if there were a certain number of passengers, but a medical student could qualify for the position at that time. In the absence of the required number of passengers, the first mate acted as ship's surgeon on this particular vessel; and he had a marvelous medicine chest. In it, for example, were the recognized medicines labeled (for combating) "Malaria," "Yellow Fever," etc., with the proper dosage indicated. The difficulty for the first mate lay in the fact that there was nothing to help him diagnose malaria, yellow fever, etc.

Pastors generally have developed the art of going beneath "the presenting problem" to sense that the real difficulty lies in, say, the counselee's love relationship. This pastoral art of diagnosing the basic problem is readily transferable to counseling in work crises wherever they may be present.

WHY IS THE COUNSELING DONE?

"And now, Israel, what does the Lord your God require of you, but to fear the Lord your God, to walk in all his ways, to love him, to serve the Lord your God with all your heart and with all your soul" (Deuteronomy 10:12).

". . . you shall love your neighbor as yourself . . ." (Leviticus 19:18*b*).

"You shall love the Lord your God with all your heart, and with all your soul, and with all your mind. This is the great and first commandment. And a second is like it, You shall love your neighbor as yourself" (Matthew 22:37-39).

In both the Law and the Prophets, loving and serving God is inseparable from loving and serving neighbors. Jesus took his place squarely within that tradition when he replied to the lawyer among the Pharisees who were testing him that these constituted the two great commandments on which all the Law and the Prophets depended.

The call of the pastor within the Judeo-Christian tradition obviously includes loving and serving both God and neighbor. When one considers what loving and serving one's neighbor implies for the pastor, it is equally obvious that it implies helping that neighbor, in turn, to love and to serve both God and neighbor as best that person can. It is no abuse of Scripture to say that the pastor's call includes helping people "work" for God and neighbor as well as for themselves, in addition to loving them. The Hebrew word, *'abad,* translated "serve" in the foregoing passage from Deuteronomy, is the same word that is translated "labor" and "work" in the fourth commandment, "Six days you shall labor, and do all your work" (Exodus 20:9; Deuteronomy 5:13). It is also the word translated "till" in the Genesis account where "the Lord God took the man and put him in the garden of Eden to till it and keep it" (Genesis 2:15).

The only things new about the pastor's call to help people in work crises are the categories of persons who need counseling now who have not needed it traditionally. One example is the widows and divorcées, who are called "the new poor" at a hearing of the United States Senate Human Resources Subcommittee on Employment, Poverty and Migratory Labor. The following article from *The Washington Post,* September 13, 1977, graphically describes their plight.

When Martha Messenger of Danville, Ill., suddenly lost her job at the age of 59 she received no severance pay, unemployment compensation or pension, even though she had worked hard for 40 years. Messenger lost her position—homemaker—when her husband asked for a divorce.

Messenger is one of millions of "displaced homemakers" thrust into the job market through divorce or death of a husband.

These women, often ill-prepared to enter the job market but in serious need of incomes, have been largely ignored by the women's movement, legislation and job placement programs, said state and national legislators, officials and educators yesterday. They endorsed a bill introduced by Sen. Birch Bayh (D-Ind.) and 18 co-sponsors that would authorize $10 million during the next fiscal year to help states establish 50 service centers to provide job training, and employment, legal and financial counseling for homemakers—"displaced" in their middle years through divorce or widowhood.

"Many recent widows and divorcees could be termed the 'new poor'," said Illinois state Rep. Susan Catania, citing the example of Messenger. Catania testified before the Senate Human Resources Subcommittee on employment, Poverty and Migratory Labor.

"Only about one divorcee in every seven is awarded alimony and less than one in two is granted financial support for the children. Many widows find that the pensions they expect to receive from their husbands' companies are a myth. Often if a husband dies before retirement, the wife is not eligible for a survivor's pension."

Bayh said one widespread myth is that all widows are financially protected at the death of their husbands by Social Security. To be eligible for Social Security a widow must be 60 years old. And if a woman is divorced before she has been married 20 years, she cannot receive dependent benefits under her former husband's Social Security.

Sen. Gaylord Nelson (D-Wis.), chairman of the Human Resources subcommittee, stated that there were no accurate estimates of the number of displaced homemakers because "no accounting has ever been made of this segment of society."

Sen. Donald W. Riegle Jr. (D-Mich.) said it is "several million and growing. There were 10 million widows in 1975—a 45 per cent increase since 1950—and 4 million divorcees—a 223 per cent increase since 1950. Over the past decade, single-parent families headed by women have grown 10 times as fast as two-parent families.

Homemakers who have spent years at unpaid jobs as wives and mothers face sex and age discrimination, emotional traumas and uncertainty when they must look for jobs, several witnesses testified at yesterday's hearing.

They are ineligible for Aid to Families with Dependent Children (AFDC), the major welfare program, if their children are over 18. They are ineligible for unemployment insurance because they have not been paid for their jobs at home. Many lose medical coverage and are not accepted in private health insurance plans, said Catania.

Thirteen states have passed bills that would help women who have never before been in the job market to find work, but state Sen. Jo Ann Maxey of Nebraska and Catania said they need federal assistance to continue and expand the programs.[11]

The women referred to as "the new poor" not only know great pain from the disruption of both their former love and work relationships, but they also have great gifts that could be used in work other than homemaking. The pastor whose eyes and ears and heart are open will know many other categories and individuals who also have the pain and the unused talents that usually accompany work crises of all kinds. Surely the pastor's call is to help them be good stewards of their talents, as well as to comfort them in their suffering.

[11] Myra MacPherson, "'The New Poor': Hill Unit Examines Plight of Widows and Divorcees," *The Washington Post*, September 13, 1977, Section A, p. 3.

Annotated Bibliography

This selective bibliography omits the titles of some books and articles cited in the text of the book. Publication information on these will be found in the notes accompanying the text where the citations occur.

Bolles, Richard N., *What Color Is Your Parachute?* Berkeley, Calif.: Ten Speed Press, 1977; paperback and cloth; the original edition of 1972 has been and is being revised and republished annually, beginning in 1975.

This is an excellent starting place for a pastor interested in work crises or for any person facing a work crisis. It also has a very full bibliography and an extensive directory of organizations, agencies, and persons offering professional help for job hunters.

————, *The Quick Job-Hunting Map.* Berkeley, Calif.: Ten Speed Press, 1976.

This booklet contains exercises that are very helpful in identifying what skills one enjoys using and where one would enjoy using them. Recommended for use by individuals and small groups. This booklet is also included in Bolles's most recent book, *The Three Boxes of Life and How to Get out of Them* (Berkeley: Ten Speed Press, 1977), as one of the tools usable in helping people blend education, work, and leisure during all the stages of life.

————, *Take Heart—A Word to the Unemployed.* Cincinnati: Forward Movement Publications, 1972, 1975.
An inexpensive, readable pamphlet which is written from a Christian point of view, *Take Heart* makes a good handout or addition to a church's "tract rack."

Caplan, Gerald, *Principles of Preventive Psychiatry.* New York: Basic Books, Inc., Publishers, 1964.
Caplan's exposition of the dynamics of crises in general is a classic in the field.

Clebsch, William, and Jaekle, Charles, *Pastoral Care in Historical Perspective*, reprint of 1964 edition. New York: Jason Aronson, Inc., 1975.
The authors trace the history and philosophy of the pastoral functions of sustaining, guiding, healing, and reconciling from the early church into the present.

Clinebell, Howard J., Jr., *Basic Types of Pastoral Counseling.* Nashville: Abingdon Press, 1966.
This single volume is an almost indispensable text on pastoral counseling in general. It also contains helpful references to other works that go more deeply into specific aspects of counseling.

Crystal, John C., and Bolles, Richard N., *Where Do I Go from Here with My Life?* New York: The Seabury Press, Inc., 1974.
The authors provide a detailed, step-by-step life-planning manual, with particular emphasis on what you want to do, where to do it, and the nature of the hiring process.

Erikson, Erik H., *Childhood and Society.* New York: W. W. Norton & Co., Inc., 1963.
Here Erikson first outlined his eight stages of human development with descriptions of the crises, the forces that produce them, and the possible resolutions for each crisis.

Holland, John L., *Making Vocational Choices: A Theory of Careers.* Englewood Cliffs, N.J.: Prentice-Hall, Inc., 1973.

This helpful book contains Holland's instrument (the Self-Directed Search) for determining the "people-environments" which individuals prefer.

Haldane, Bernard H., *How to Make a Habit of Success.* Washington, D.C.: Acropolis Books, 1975.
Haldane, a pioneer in the field of career guidance, first published this landmark book in 1960; it is still valuable.

————, *Career Satisfaction and Success: A Guide to Job Freedom.* New York: AMACOM, a division of American Management Associations, 1974.
This is a combination work and textbook, which presents an opportunity to utilize his "System to Identify Motivated Skills," referred to as "SIMS."

Lathrop, Richard, *Who's Hiring Who*, 3rd rev. ed. Berkeley: Ten Speed Press, 1977.
Help is provided here for new job hunters by describing the steps they should consider taking in their search.

Newsletter. Walnut Creek, Calif.: The National Career Development Project of United Ministries in Higher Education. Published six times yearly.
Richard N. Bolles is editor of this bulletin which contains reviews of current books published in the field of career guidance and thoughtful articles by the editor.

Schwed, Peter, *Hanging In There: How to Resist Retirement from Life & Avoid Being Put Out to Pasture.* Boston: Houghton Mifflin Co., 1977.
This is a sprightly, entertaining book designed to animate those who are retired or facing retirement. There are also lively illustrations by Whitney Darrow, Jr., long-time cartoonist for the *New Yorker* magazine.

Sheehy, Gail, *Passages.* New York: E. P. Dutton, 1976.
The great popularity of this book is well deserved. It concentrates on the transitional stage of midlife but is not restricted to that. The numerous case histories provide helpful data.

Wedel, Theodore O., *The Gospel in a Strange, New World.* Philadelphia: The Westminster Press, 1963.

Published here are the Kellogg Lectures which Wedel delivered in 1962 at the Episcopal Divinity School, Cambridge, Massachusetts. They provide a remarkably clear statement of his "relationship" theology.

————, *The Drama of the Bible*. Cincinnati: Forward Movement Publications, 1965.

This little book, now in its fourth printing, contains five informal lectures which the author delivered in 1955. It presents the full sweep of the biblical drama as a "story" in which people can place themselves today.

Index